The
GOAL
Formula

ERIK THERWANGER

The
GOAL
Formula

Completing the Big Picture of Your Life

BALBOA.
PRESS

A DIVISION OF HAY HOUSE

Balboa Press books may be ordered through booksellers or by contacting:

Balboa Press
A Division of Hay House
1663 Liberty Drive
Bloomington, IN 47403
www.balboapress.com
1 (877) 407-4847

Print information available on the last page.

ISBN: 978-1-9822-1298-8 (sc)
ISBN: 978-1-9822-1300-8 (hc)
ISBN: 978-1-9822-1299-5 (e)

Library of Congress Control Number: 2018911873

Balboa Press rev. date: 11/29/2018

Dedicated to:

*My wife, Gina, for using The GOAL Formula to accomplish
our goals, during all of your battles with cancer.*

*My fellow U.S. Marines, your ability to accomplish
any mission, while maintaining the highest level of
integrity, is still the foundation of my life.*

*Those of you who are ready to accomplish your goals and achieve a
greater life, no matter what circumstances you face. Your desire to
take your life to the next level has inspired me to write this book.*

Contents

Introduction

Create a Sense of Urgency

Greatness is for anyone who chooses to Think GREAT!

"Marine Recruit Training is No Rose Garden." Those were the words on a brochure that was given to me by my recruiter when I was seventeen years old. It was 100% correct. Boot camp was challenging, every day, all day long. For 90 days, we were trained by four intensely focused, hard-charging drill instructors. Their orders were to transform a group of civilians into United States Marines. Platoon 1095 started out with 75 recruits, but only 46 would accomplish the goal of graduating on November 13, 1987.

Boot camp is a series of extreme conditions, both physical and mental. To accomplish our goal, we needed to complete dozens of tasks, despite our circumstances. Failure was not an option, for those who wanted to graduate. Our drill instructors guaranteed that we were not handed the title of Marine, we had to earn it.

Within 90 days, I qualified with my rifle, passed exams, negotiated obstacle courses, completed inspections, learned to rappel, and ran three miles in just over eighteen minutes. That's just to name a few. The goal of graduating boot camp helped me to fulfill a greater purpose – I became a Marine. My goal was merely part of a bigger picture.

Most people want to accomplish goals, but they often feel like they are in boot camp. They have important goals in their lives, but the physical and mental challenges they encounter often get in the way of their goals. I am going to show you the formula to accomplish your goals – no matter what circumstances you face!

I graduated boot camp over 20 years ago, but that brief, 90-day period, forever changed my view of accomplishing goals. I wrote this book for one reason – to help you combine the necessary elements to accomplish any goal you desire. As you may have guessed, I'm a goal-oriented person. I've set small goals, big goals, fun goals, and life-changing goals. In fact, the only thing I like better than setting goals, is accomplishing them.

I've found that most people are good at setting goals, but usually fail at accomplishing them. Goal-setting is a lot like dreaming. Writing down your goals always starts off with a lot of excitement and unlimited possibilities. Accomplishing them, however, is often a different story.

Have you ever experienced the positive feeling of setting an amazing, life-changing goal, then felt like the events in your life sucked the wind right out of your sails? I have. I experienced a five-year period of time, that was filled with some of the toughest challenges I have ever faced.

I was shook to the core of my foundation and nearly tossed in the towel on my goals. I had just finalized a divorce from my first marriage of eight years. I went from seeing my sons every night to every other weekend. Soon after, I was laid off from my job and started to accrue back child support – with interest.

I did, however, meet Gina during this time. She was a unique, amazing woman with a real zest for life. We dated for three years then married on a beautiful Halloween day in 1998. Ten months later, she was diagnosed with an aggressive form of cancer; Non-Hodgkin's Lymphoma. She was quickly admitted to a hospital and would be starting her chemotherapy treatments. Everything was spinning out of control.

Just before she received her first chemotherapy treatment, Gina's oncologist pulled me aside and encouraged me to keep her spirits high. If you're thinking that it was tough to keep her spirits high during this time, you are absolutely correct! We were newlyweds, lived in a small apartment, and did not have a dime in savings.

I tried everything to keep her positive. A little bit of humor seemed to help, but I often ran out of jokes. Visits from family members worked too, but sometimes she did not feel like having any guests. We needed something more than a temporary fix. The chemotherapy made her violently ill and she slept most of the time. One day, as I sat at the edge of her hospital bed,, I discovered the solution; a permanent solution to keeping her positive.

We started to talk about buying a home. Gina lit up. Her crystal-blue eyes sparkled again. I had not seen that in weeks. Well, I was definitely onto something. We set the goal of buying a home, right there on her bed. She was bald and weak, but her spirits were high.

We talked about what the house would look like, how we were going to decorate the rooms, and what types of flowers would be planted in the backyard. We set other goals too. We wanted to build a nest egg, eliminate debt, and travel the world. We wanted to enjoy life. But setting our goals would only provide Gina with a temporary feeling of satisfaction. I needed her to experience the permanent sensation of accomplishing them. Failure was not an option.

With everything going on, I needed a guarantee that we would hit our goals. We not only had life-changing goals to accomplish, but we had life-saving goals to help us make it through these tough times. Unable to continue working, Gina was placed on disability, which did not help our finances. As her caregiver, I searched for a position that would allow me to earn an income and provide me the extensive amount of time off I needed, in order to take care of her.

Because of my 3-hour daily commute, I left my job in the entertainment industry. In fact, I had just started working there a week before Gina had been diagnosed. I found an opportunity in the financial services industry, selling financial products. I had absolutely no background in sales and I was now being paid on commission only. We continued to focus on the goals we had set, but the times got a little tougher. Sometimes, it felt like our current situation made boot camp seem easy!

We accumulated debt, lost our vehicle, and our utilities were shut off – several times! After a full year of treatments, Gina's cancer did go into remission. But a few weeks later, she was forced to go back into the City of Hope due to complications from all of the treatments she had received. We tried our best to get back to a normal life, but six months later, my father passed away.

It took nearly two years of recovery for Gina to get her full strength back. It's hard to fully express how difficult these times were, but you probably have an idea. The thought of accomplishing goals, at this time in our lives, often seemed impossible, but I knew the positive effects that they would have on our lives and Gina's survival.

My life certainly was no rose garden at that moment, but our goals were important to us. It was during this time that I created *The GOAL Formula*. My tour of duty in the Marine Corps introduced me to the basic components of *The GOAL Formula*, but I truly discovered the importance of applying it when I was Gina's caregiver.

The GOAL Formula helps you put together the elements necessary to accomplishing your goals. It is based on two unique disciplines: the duties of a U.S. Marine and the responsibilities of a caregiver. You're probably thinking that these two areas have nothing in common with one another. Through the course of this book, I will show you how you can utilize the survival techniques and strategies of both, to accomplish any goal – without going to boot camp, or to a hospital!

Most people struggle with their goals because they do not understand the basic, simple elements to accomplish them. Even without challenges, many people stop moving toward their goals within two weeks of setting them. They tend to set the same goals, over and over. They become professional goal-setters, but never experience the results of hitting their goals. Do you know anyone like that?

By following a proven formula for accomplishing your goals, you can change your life, no matter what you are faced with. When my life was filled with more obstacles, hardships, and stress than I thought possible, I applied the formula and accomplished my goals. I increased my income by over 500% and eliminated debt. I bought my first home and rental properties. I changed careers and started my own company. But, most importantly, I achieved a greater life. That's what accomplishing goals is all about – experiencing the life you have always dreamt about.

Yes, life can get in the way, but it doesn't have to stop you from realizing your dreams. Perhaps you are at a point in your life that is "no rose garden." It should not stop you from accomplishing your goals. In fact, it is often during these times, that it is more important to accomplish them.

Accomplishing your goals is all about combining the right elements. I call it *The GOAL Formula*:

- **The 5 Steps**
- **Time**
- **People**

I was not about to give up on my wife, our marriage, our family, or our goals. This book is an account of the formula I used, during some difficult times, to achieve a greater life.

I encourage you to use the same formula to accomplish your goals as well. You will never move forward by standing still. Accomplish your goals, starting today!

Think GREAT,

Erik

Part I

The Big Picture

Part I

The Big Picture

Get a Clear Picture of your Goals!

Perception is everything. How you perceive something directly impacts how you accomplish something. Too often, people set out to accomplish goals, and that's it. They jot down items they wish to accomplish, get off to a strong start, but quickly fizzle. It's unfortunate, because many of these unaccomplished goals would have been life-changing.

People easily give up on great goals, like losing weight, making more money, switching to a better career, and creating a happier family-life. When trying to accomplish your goals without having the right perception, you can lose focus and stop prematurely. Has this ever happened to you? It happens to a lot of people, every year. Each year, millions of people set New Year's Resolutions, but never *resolve* anything. Next year, they set the same resolutions. The year after that... well, you get the picture.

I accomplish goals because I view them as a piece of the puzzle to my *Big Picture*. With that in mind, developing your bigger picture will help to accomplish your goals. Every goal you set is a necessary piece of an important puzzle. One that will help you to experience a greater life when the pieces are connected. Remember, graduating boot camp was my goal, but becoming a Marine was part of my big picture.

Connecting your goals will allow you to gain a complete picture of the life you desire and deserve. In addition to constantly working on achieving greatness in my life, I also work with many others who want to accomplish life-changing goals. Although each goal is unique, they all fall somewhere into five unique categories.

THE FANTASTIC FIVE

Accomplishing goals in one or more of these areas will help you to have a life that is *remarkable in magnitude and degree*. For most people, their definition of greatness can be found within the Fantastic Five.

FAITH – Goals that allow you to pursue spiritual growth. Accomplishing *Faith* goals will allow you to rise beyond the purely material world and find a truer balance in your life.

FAMILY – Goals that enhance the meaningful relationships in your life. Accomplishing *Family* goals will give you a deeper feeling of love and belonging.

FINANCIAL – Goals that involve building a career, increasing income, eliminating debt, and building financial security. Accomplishing *Financial* goals will allow you to build stability and have peace of mind.

FITNESS – Goals that involve improving your health through nutrition and exercise. Accomplishing *Fitness* goals will allow you to live a longer, more enjoyable life.

FUN – Goals that involve your personal interests. Accomplishing your *Fun* goals will add a new level of excitement to your life.

Imagine how empowered you would feel to accomplish goals within one of these areas! Now imagine accomplishing goals in all of these areas! When you improve your life in one of these areas, it always gives you the confidence to start improving the others.

When Gina was battling cancer, I was constantly out in the field trying to sell. I met with clients later in the evening and was always on the go. I rarely ate at home because the mere smell of food made Gina sick. I found myself skipping meals or grabbing some unhealthy fast-food. Over time, I had gained a lot of weight. The Marine Corps would not have recognized me.

I used *The GOAL Formula* to accomplish my weight loss goal (Fitness). In 90 days, I had dropped 42 pounds! Accomplishing this goal gave me the energy to accomplish the goal of writing my first book (Fun). I had more energy to play with my daughter and spend quality time with the people I care most about (Family). I performed better at work and hit more sales goals (Financial). There were so many benefits that came with accomplishing my one goal of losing weight. My life was greater because my Big Picture was taking shape.

There is really just one purpose for accomplishing goals; to experience the positive impact they have on your life and the lives of those you care about. Many people stop trying to accomplish their goals because they never create the big picture of what a greater life would look like. Can you put together a puzzle without looking at the picture on the box? Sure, but it is much more difficult.

I always look at the box cover. Why? Because I want an edge. By creating the big picture of your life, you create an edge for accomplishing your goals. By not painting a picture of the life you need, you limit your ability to accomplish your goals. Accomplishing one goal always increases your chances of accomplishing another goal, just as I did through my weight loss goal.

Based on where you are in your life, your big picture may change as time goes by. When Gina and I were going through her first battle with cancer, our big picture was about gaining a sense of control in our lives. Our goals focused on building financial security and family stability. Today, our big picture involves helping others to accomplish their goals. As our big picture expands, we make sure that our goals are in alignment with that image.

Creating your big picture is an amazing experience and will empower you to set and accomplish life-changing goals.

Here are three powerful components that will help you to develop a crystal-clear Big Picture:

1. Your Definition of GREAT
2. Your Definition of a Greater Life
3. Your Greater Purpose

There's a big difference between good and great . There are a lot of definitions of great, but I have always used one that helps me to add clarity to my Big Picture.

My Definition of GREAT:

Life-changing and remarkable in magnitude and degree.

What is your definition of great?

To increase your chances of accomplishing your goals, identify what a *greater life* means to you.

My Definition of a Greater Life:

To provide my family with support, guidance, and love that will enable them to build meaningful relationships, enjoy life, and fulfill their greater purpose.

What is your definition of a greater life?

A greater life is absolutely attainable, no matter what your personal circumstances are. By defining your greater purpose, (why you are here), your goals will take on a new, deeper meaning. This may require some deeper thought, but it is well worth the effort you put into it.

My Greater Purpose:

To help people to accomplish their goals – no matter what circumstances they face.

What is your Greater Purpose?

If you are not able to clearly define all three right now, don't worry. You can always come back to this page and enhance your definitions.

All of my goals, big and small, are linked to my greater purpose. I defined my greater purpose in July of 2000. I was at the City of Hope, visiting with Gina when I had a life-changing moment. A moment that continues to guide me to this day.

Gina was at her lowest point of her cancer treatments. She was admitted to City of Hope to try one last procedure. If it didn't work, we were told that she would "not be here next year." She was waiting to receive a stem cell transplant. But her white blood cell count was too low for them to administer the treatment. She was not only waiting, she was dying.

Placed in a sterile room, I had to scrub down and wear a face mask each time I visited her. As we were sitting in her room, a young man stepped in and said, "I was in this room one year ago. I had Non-Hodgkin's Lymphoma. I lived and so will you." He never gave his name, but Gina and I will never forget the few words he spoke. Her spirits were lifted with the hope and inspiration he gave her. Her white blood cell count rose, and she soon received her transplant.

From that moment on, my greater purpose became crystal clear.

A BOOK WITH A GOAL

What is the problem with most self-help books? They always look brand new, even after they have been read. *The GOAL Formula* is designed specifically for you to read it, study it, and apply it, to the areas of your life you most want to improve. This is not a *how-to* book, but rather a *how-you* book, focusing on empowering the one person who can guarantee that you will accomplish your goals – You!

The GOAL Formula is divided into four powerful sections, paying careful attention to the parts necessary to get the results you need. It is designed to get you started, to stay on track, and to accomplish the goals required to experience a new level of achievement in your life.

Part I: The Big Picture – Helps you to develop your Big Picture and details the five steps to accomplish any goal.

Part II: Time Mastery – Teaches you how to structure your time, especially during the next 90 days, so you are prepared to complete the big picture of your life.

Part III: You Never Run Alone – Shows you the benefits of incorporating other people into your journey to accomplish your life-changing goals.

Part IV: Your 90 Day Run Starts Now – Provides you with templates to create your own Goal Planning Strategy (G.P.S.), which will keep you on track to see your goals all the way through.

By learning *The GOAL Formula*, you will start to accomplish your most important goals, in less time than you ever thought possible.

Chapter 1

It's Time to Think G.R.E.A.T.

Take the Steps to a Greater Life!

A *Dream* is something you wish for. A *Goal* is something you strive for. An *Accomplishment* is something you complete. Why do most people feel incomplete? Most people feel that way because they have few accomplishments in their lives.

Everyone wants to take control of their lives and accomplish their goals. People focus on experiencing greater health, enhancing relationships, improving finances, developing their spiritual journey, and enjoying new levels of success. Business owners want to accomplish goals too. Improving sales, creating better leadership teams, and elevating company profits top the list.

In America alone, the desire to accomplish life-changing goals is mind-blowing. Each year, millions of dollars are spent by individuals and organizations on personal and professional development. Here is a breakdown of what Americans spend on taking control of their lives.

Marketdata Enterprises states:

In 2005, the total self-improvement market was estimated to be $9.59 billion. It is expected that the market will grow by more than 11% per year through 2010. That would put it close to $14 billion in annual spending!

- Books $693 million
- Audio Books $2.08 billion
- Weight loss programs $3.97 billion

With this much money being spent to improve lives, why do we see so few people with better lives? Quite simply, people pay for the cost of a greater life, but rarely pay the price to experience it. Approximately 12 million Americans are involved in nearly 500,000 self-help programs.

There is nothing wrong with investing in some good resources to improve your life, but do not confuse paying for someone's books or programs with guaranteeing your results. A greater life requires a different price. Throughout history, people achieved greatness without the assistance of self-help programs. They did it without access to all of our current resources, and they often faced extreme challenges, too. So, how did they do it? They made the choice to take control of their lives – they made the choice to Think G.R.E.A.T.

- **Think** – Control your *thoughts*
- **G.R.E.A.T.** – Control your *actions*

ALWAYS THINK G.R.E.A.T.

During our five-year period of challenges, a lot of things appeared to be out of my control. Handling Gina's health issues, her treatments, our finances, and my career, all felt like being on a high-speed roller coaster; one that never slowed down. Adding goals to this ride seemed impractical, until I discovered that I was always in control of my thoughts and actions.

I made the decision to *Think G.R.E.A.T.*, regardless of how fast our roller coaster was traveling, or how many sharp turns came our way. As for my thoughts, I was committed to keeping a positive attitude, an unwavering mindset, and a high belief level to realize our big picture.

As for my actions, I was more than willing to be in control of them, but I needed to identify them first. I discovered that every goal can be accomplished if you take the right steps. As I looked more into the true meaning of greatness, I found the first element of *The Goal Formula*.

The 5 Steps to Accomplishing Goals:

1. Identify important **G**oals in your life...**G**
2. Establish powerful **R**easons for accomplishing your goals...............**R**
3. Set high **E**xpectations for yourself...**E**
4. Take all of the **A**ctions necessary to achieve a greater life...............**A**
5. Track your results intensely...**T**

SEARCHING FOR "G.R.E.A.T."

Success leaves clues, if you are looking for them. To make money in my new sales career, I started to pay close attention to the successful sales associates in my office. Roughly 20% of our sales team out-earned the other 80%. At first glance, these top producers seemed to be 'naturals' at making money. How could I create the same results when selling was so unnatural for me? I was amazed to learn that many of them had been at 'rock-bottom' at least once in their careers. They not only weathered the storm, but they reached new levels of success.

I needed results like theirs, so I looked deeper into their success stories. I quickly became less impressed with their actual achievements and more fascinated in how they managed to do it. I began to identify some common denominators that they each shared. Common 'steps' that I could apply to my sales efforts and to my life.

To my surprise, I discovered that their success was not based on their sales skills or even their financial services training, although both helped. In fact, the successful sales associates were not the most knowledgeable ones in the office. But they earned the most! What separated them from the rest? What allowed these people to achieve different results?

The biggest surprise, which made no sense to me at the time, was that they seemed to work less hours than the others in our office. Because of my responsibilities on the home front with Gina, I liked the idea of working less and making more. Actually, I have never met anyone who did not like that idea!

The successful sales associates used the same presentation materials, the same day planner and even attended the same training as all of the other associates. But their results were significantly different. Everyone in the office set sales goals; they accomplished them. Because of that, they had more confidence, a higher sense of self-esteem, and were generally more excited about life. Accomplishing their sales goals allowed them to make more money.

I needed to know how they accomplished their goals. As I continued to invest more time with them, the light finally switched on and I understood what truly separated them from the rest. It was obvious the whole time. They did not try and hide it and they actually made it easy for everyone to see. They meticulously followed the five steps to accomplishing goals, every day.

"G.R.E.A.T." REVEALED

The first step I noticed was in their offices. Each of these 'superstars' had their goals posted, in plain sight. And not just their sales goals like "make more calls," or "be number one for the month." Those goals were posted too. But they had deeper goals posted, like "retire my wife," "trip to Hawaii with the family," "become debt-free," and "build an education fund for Jennifer." These goals had real meaning. In fact, they actually got me excited, and they were not even my goals.

Pictures were also posted, as reminders of 'why' they were striving for their goals. Next to the "retire my wife" goal was a picture of his wife. Next to the "start education fund for Jennifer" goal was a picture of her beautiful 3-year-old daughter. They knew 'why' they were pursuing their goals. I began to think more about the reasons why I needed to accomplish my goals.

They also knew exactly when they were going to accomplish these goals and what resources were required of them, to do so. They had dates (timelines) attached to each of their goals. It was obvious that the accomplishment of their goals was 100% their responsibility. Their expectations greatly exceeded everyone else's.

They were people of action, moving at a faster pace than the others. Procrastination was not part of their plan. They had a purpose and a sense of urgency in everything they did. They followed the right steps, every day, to accomplish their goals.

To exceed their goals, which they often did, they focused intensely on tracking their results. The other 80% in our office avoided accountability like the plague. The successful team members carefully monitored their progress to increase their results. They reported their performance numbers in meetings, and they put their names on the 'big board,' showing their potential business to everyone. They did not hide behind their challenges or make excuses.

THINK G.R.E.A.T. NOW

Successful people put the spotlight on themselves and turn the heat all the way up. All eyes are on them, and that is exactly what they want. It is never a surprise to see them succeed. Control your thoughts and actions and you will achieve a greater life, no matter what circumstances you face.

Most people regularly make a trip to the grocery store to re-stock their house. Too often, this was not the case for us. Asking Gina to hold off on buying groceries, while she was receiving cancer treatments, was not one of my better techniques for 'keeping her spirits high.'

One of the most important goals I had was to increase my sales and earn more money. Our entire livelihood relied on my commissions, but early in my sales career, I found that my money ended before my month ended. It was during this time that I became laser-focused on learning to Think GREAT. When I controlled my thoughts and actions, I increased my chances of accomplishing any goal I set.

As I discovered how to maximize the impact of each step, I applied them to my sales efforts, helping me to become a top producer and recruiter. Identifying the five steps was important, but during our toughest times, I needed to intimately understand how each step worked.

No matter what steps you take in life, your thoughts will determine how far you get. The distance you travel is always determined by the limits of your thoughts. Did Gina and I ever get depressed, sad, or frustrated on our journey? Yes, absolutely. We had a lot going on. But we made the choice to think differently and follow the five steps.

Let's take a closer look at each step.

Chapter 2

G – Goals

Identify Important Goals in Your Life!

What is a goal? A goal is a defined dream with a powerful plan. Dreams that are truly important to you will find their way out of your head and onto paper. I have found that just by starting to focus on your goals, you will begin to improve your life.

When was the last time you found yourself dreaming *big*? The kind of dreams you had when you were young and felt as if you could conquer the world. When I was young, I dreamed of being an astronaut and flying into space. At some point in my life, I had the sad realization that my dreaming had stopped. The reality of life seemed to have pushed my dreams farther and farther away, or should I say, back down to earth.

Think back for a moment, to when you were young, and you were dreaming big.

Answer the following questions with a YES or NO:

Did your life turn out the way you thought it would?   _____

Are you the person you thought you would be?   _____

Have you accomplished what you thought you would?   _____

It is sad, but most people stop dreaming. Many give up and settle for mediocrity. Others give up on their dreams because they failed to accomplish important goals in their past. People who stop dreaming, stop living life to the fullest!

Maybe your goals have changed, or perhaps you have abandoned them because of the demands of your current situation. Are you ready to reengage your life? Goal setting is exciting because you get to dream again! Here is the promising news: not only do you get to start dreaming again, but this time, you also get to take the proven steps to transforming your dreams into realities. As you work on accomplishing goals and achieving a greater life, you will improve your self-esteem, confidence, and enthusiasm about life. You will start to look forward to each day and what each day will bring to you.

THE ROLE OF TASKS

In order to accomplish your goals, there will be many tasks associated with them. Tasks make up the individual duties required for accomplishing each of your life-changing goals. But there is a significant difference between your goals and your tasks.

Tasks are necessary assignments, which need to be completed to accomplish your goals. Most people feel burdened by assignments, usually associating them with chores. Goals are not chores. They are sources of inspiration, which need to be accomplished in order to achieve a greater life and complete your big picture.

Imagine having a beautiful yard for your children to play in. One that would allow you to entertain family and friends. A place where you can enhance your personal relationships, or just relax and enjoy a beautiful sunset. Having an amazing backyard is a great goal, but the task of planting and maintaining the grass is one of the necessary 'chores' associated with creating that yard. If you treat your goals as chores, you turn their excitement into drudgery.

There is a notable difference between accomplishing goals and completing tasks. While most people find a sense of satisfaction after a task has been completed, that feeling is usually temporary and quickly fades away.

Goals are different. The satisfaction gained from accomplishing a goal always lasts longer. And there is another significant difference. You do not have to wait until a goal is accomplished to receive the full benefit from that goal. You will not only enhance your personal performance once the goal has been accomplished, but your performance will actually increase during the process of striving toward your goals.

THE IMPACT OF GOALS

Goal setting can mean the difference between having a life and truly living. In order to be considered a goal, it must be written down. Remember, goals which are not written down, stay in dreamland. Trying to accomplish goals that are not written down is like building a house without blueprints. The mere act of transferring your goals to paper causes great momentum.

Goals impact performance! In fact, when you pursue goals in one area of your life, your performance in other areas tends to improve as well. People have used the process of goal setting throughout history to accomplish greatness. The Seven Wonders of the World must have begun as written goals, even if they happened to be written in the sand.

In the mid-1960's, Professor Edwin A. Locke, a psychologist at the University of Maryland, College Park, began to examine the idea of goal setting as a means of increasing productivity. His goal setting theory is regarded as one of the most widely-respected theories in industrial-organizational psychology. Locke proved that goal setting increases personal performance. He invested thirty years of his life to researching this idea. More than 2000 years before Locke, Aristotle proclaimed that there were four main causes of nature and declared that purpose can cause action. In other words, goals cause people to move.

Goals give you an edge! The mere fact of pursuing a goal stimulates personal growth. The more difficult the goal, the greater the increase will be.

Having goals will help you in three main areas:

1. Your attention will become laser-focused.
2. Your productivity will increase.
3. You will become more persistent.

Setting goals and achieving goals are two completely different functions.

WHY PEOPLE AVOID SETTING GOALS

I believe that writing down a goal requires commitment. Many people will not take that first step, because they are not *prepared* to take the remaining steps. Fear is one of the primary reasons for not setting goals. Your perception of fear determines how you handle fear. I choose to perceive it as nothing more than: False Evidence Appearing Real.

Understanding the basic fears associated with goal-setting will help you to overcome them.

Fear of CRITICISM

Many people fear being criticized by others. It is easy to find fault with others, especially for those who have no interest in improving their own lives. Those without goals are more comfortable to see you settle for an average life, along with them.

• Stop focusing on what others think and start to Think G.R.E.A.T.

Fear of FAILURE

No one has ever achieved greatness without first experiencing some level of failure. Thomas Edison failed over 10,000 times before discovering how to make the incandescent light bulb work. But, Edison was quoted as saying that he did not fail, he just found 10,000 ways that it did not work.

You can expect some failures before accomplishing your goals, just as someone in the sales profession will experience 'No' many times before hearing 'Yes.'

• Change your perception of failure and 'fail' your way to a greater life!

Fear of SUCCESS

As odd as it sounds, people fear success; even those who pursue it. Some feel guilty and believe that they do not deserve it, while others believe that even after achieving it, they still will not be happy. Others believe that if they achieve success, they will not be able to hold onto it. These self-defeating thoughts take away the belief in their own abilities, preventing them from trying to accomplish their goals.

- Become successful so you can help others!

GOALS GIVE HOPE

During Gina's battle with cancer, the goal of buying our own home was still important, although it did not always feel like a reality. We lived in a small apartment. Shortly after Gina was diagnosed, her mom moved in to help out. We were struggling financially, our home was cramped, and we rarely left the apartment as a couple. Buying a home seemed impossible.

Gina's final treatment occurred at the City of Hope. They performed a stem cell transplant. After a thirty day stay, in a sterile room, Gina returned home. She had very little energy and slept most of the day. During her year of treatments, everything was very regimented. We knew when her doctor appointments were, exactly when her treatments were, and even knew when she would get sick from the chemotherapy. After the treatment phase, we expected to regain some normalcy back in our lives.

We were about to discover that the recovery phase would be anything but regimented. Gina had been prescribed many different medications. At one point, we had over 20 different prescriptions on our bathroom counter. As you can imagine, the effect on her body and mind was not pleasant.

We were focused on that home, so we took our written goal and posted it on the mirror in our bathroom, right next to Gina's medication. This gave us the opportunity to see that goal many times, every day. But to us, it was so much more than just a piece of paper on our mirror. It was our first step toward a greater life.

Gina perked up whenever we talked about our 'house,' so we focused on it more! The more we focused on our goal, the more energy she got. We knew that accomplishing this goal would be *life-changing and remarkable in magnitude and degree* for our family. Nothing was going to stop us from accomplishing it.

We viewed that goal every day, on paper, until we finally walked through the front door of our own home. Our goal had become a reality. In 2004, we bought our first home! That night, we fired up the spa, and took a well-deserved rest. We took all five steps to accomplish this goal, starting with Step 1: Identify important goals in your life.

HOW DO GOALS HELP ME TO SEE MY BIG PICTURE?

There is only one purpose for setting your goals and that is to accomplish them. Accomplishing your goals will transform your life from 'settling' to 'soaring.' When you are ready to have a greater life, start setting powerful goals. Keep in mind that goal setting is much more than merely jotting down things you want, as you did when you were young, and you filled out a birthday 'wish' list. That may have worked when you were a kid, but accomplishing anything significant takes dedication, discipline, and determination.

THE 3 C'S – KEYS TO EFFECTIVE GOAL SETTING

When I set goals, I have found that there are three key factors for increasing my odds of accomplishing them. Incorporate these three aspects into your goal-setting process.

1. Be Clear
2. Be Challenging
3. Be Certain

Be CLEAR

The more specific you can be about your goals, the more likely you are to accomplish them. One of the most common goals set every year is losing weight. For many people, this goal is of the highest priority, and for good reason. It is estimated that 127 million adults in the U.S. are overweight. In fact, many people need to lose weight due to their health conditions. For some, losing weight can save their lives.

There is no question why weight loss is at the top of so many lists. If this goal is so important, and so many people write it down, why do so few accomplish it? The goal that most people write down is, "lose weight." This is a vague goal and causes a small level of commitment. Be more specific about your goals.

When I set my goal of losing weight, I first wrote down "I need to lose 16 pounds." I was 216 pounds, so the goal of getting back down to 200 pounds was important. I gave myself 90 days to hit that goal. By having a clearly defined goal, and following the remaining steps, I lost the 16 pounds in thirty days.

- The more specific you are, the higher your commitment level is and you will increase your chances of accomplishing your goal.

Be CHALLENGING

People respond better to goals that have some level of difficulty to them. By making your goals slightly more challenging, you will actually increase your chances of accomplishing them. During my 90 days to losing weight, I realized that I was going to accomplish my first goal of losing 16 pounds, so I increased the scope of my goal. I decided to lose 20 pounds, then 25, then 30. I continued to challenge myself.

By the end of my 90 days, I had not only lost the 16 pounds, but shed an additional 26 pounds. My total weight loss was 42 pounds in 90 days.

- Challenging goals cause you to tap into your undiscovered potential.

Be CERTAIN

Your goals should cause a sense of unwavering determination within you. Working toward your goals will create momentum and excitement, both of which will increase your effectiveness in other areas of your life. Without a well-defined destination in mind, most people either stand still or soon find that they are traveling in the wrong direction, which explains why so many people get off track, or easily give up.

Certainty will keep you on track. As I started to lose weight, I became more certain that I could lose more. My confidence increased, and I soon felt that my goal had no choice but to be accomplished.

- You do not need to have a 100% perfect plan to accomplish goals. Your plan will develop along the way.

TWO TYPES OF GOALS

To achieve a greater life, I divide my goals into two simple categories:

1. **Short-Term** – those you can accomplish in a 90-day period.
2. **Long-Term** – those which require more than 90 days to accomplish.

Accomplishing both your short-term goals and long-term goals will be important to achieving a greater life. Both types of goals provide you with clarity and direction.

Short-Term

Short-term goals give you the immediate motivation necessary to accomplish your long-term goals. These 'smaller' goals provide you with the needed excitement to stay the course because you can accomplish them within 90 days. People who accomplish great things have mastered the art of taking small steps by breaking their larger goals into smaller achievable ones.

Long-Term

Long-term goals help you to overcome short-term obstacles. These larger goals provide your overall direction and will point out the way to a greater life.

Our goal of buying a home was a long-term goal. We knew it would take more than 90 days, so we broke it down into short-term goals. Improving credit scores, saving money for a down payment, and building a relationship with a realtor were goals we could accomplish in a 90-day period.

Some goals can seem overwhelmingly large. How do you eat an elephant? Just like anything else, one bite at a time. Big dreams are easier to accomplish when they are broken down into smaller steps. One of the main reasons that people do not achieve their goals is that they seem too daunting, too big. Life-changing goals are easier to accomplish if they are broken into short-term goals.

Most of today's successful companies have incorporated goal setting into their business models to improve the performance of their employees. They focus on everything from productivity to employee morale. Imagine the increase in your own productivity and morale as you incorporate goal setting into your personal life.

STEP 1: IDENTIFY IMPORTANT GOALS IN YOUR LIFE

Let's get this book dirty and take the first step together. Do not hold back. Choose goals that are *life-changing and remarkable in magnitude and degree* for you.

Here are few tips to help set important goals:

- Spend time thinking about your big picture.
- Read your definition of Great, a Greater Life, and your Greater Purpose.
- Review the Fantastic Five – goals from each category will complement each other.
- Be Clear, Challenging, and Certain.

Step 1: Identify three important goals in your life

Goal 1:_____

Goal 2:_____

Goal 3:_____

Congratulations on taking the first step. Every page of this book is designed to help you accomplish your goals and see your big picture.

Chapter 3

R – Reasons

Establish Powerful Reasons for Accomplishing Your Goals!

A goal without a reason is like a car without an engine. Writing down a goal is never enough to accomplish it. Just look at all of the New Year's resolutions we make every year. One of the most popular reoccurring goals is to get in shape. But most workout programs focus only on the goal itself: 'Lose Weight.' Too often, *why* the weight needs to be lost is ignored and people soon fall off track.

Most people get excited about listing their resolutions. So why is it they stop trying to accomplish them so quickly? The strength of your reasons determines your success. When you attempt to accomplish goals without reasons to motivate yourself, you lose focus. A goal is more easily abandoned if strong reasons for its accomplishment are not attached to it.

Whenever you attempt to accomplish something great, life has a unique way of putting obstacles in your path. Every time I have set goals, I have encountered a challenge in my life, sometimes multiple challenges. Remember that tough times come, and you need to have strong reasons to weather the storm. Strong reasons crystallize your goals.

Gina and I found that having a goal was never enough to get us through the challenging times. The reasons behind our goals provided us with the strength to overcome our obstacles. Writing your dreams down on paper is like transplanting a tree. But, without its roots, the tree will not survive. And neither will your goals without their reasons!

There are thousands of books about setting and accomplishing goals. But very few discuss the power of focusing on your reasons for achieving them. *Why* you are doing something is always more important than *what* you are doing. If you do not have inspiring and motivating reasons, your goals are nothing more than words on a page.

THE IMPACT OF REASONS

Your *why* paves your *way*. A GREAT life does not happen by accident. There are *reasons* why some people are able to accomplish their goals and others are not. Everyone uses a certain amount of energy to get through each day. Strong reasons will help convert that energy into power.

By attaching strong reasons to your goals, you will produce far greater results than the day-to-day reactive efforts of people not striving for a greater life. How you focus your energy on a daily basis will determine how much you accomplish. It is amazing how fast a day goes by and so much of your energy remains unused on your goals.

Each day, the sun delivers millions of kilowatts of solar energy, most of which is unused by us as a source of power. It is estimated that the solar energy the earth receives every three days more than matches the estimated total of all the fossil fuels on earth!

The sun has provided this abundance of energy every day for over 5 billion years. Imagine what our world would be like if we turned a fraction of that energy into power. Your reasons will enable you to turn your personal energy into personal power, in much the same way a magnifying glass can focus the energy of the sun into a powerful beam of light. That focused beam can start a fire. Of course, that light needs to be aimed (Action – Chapter 5) at the right materials to cause combustion, but you see the point!

Most goals, especially significant ones, create a great sense of pleasure, self-worth, and empowerment when accomplished. Your goals will also present you with an equal amount of challenges, obstacles, and headaches. Strong reasons will give you the power to push through these roadblocks.

Some of the challenges you face may seem to knock you down from time to time. But your reasons will pick you back up and get yourself onto your feet. You cannot take steps to a greater life if you stay on the ground! A big *why* will help you tackle any *how* that stands in your way. Strong reasons not only give you the power to accomplish your goals, they can enhance your ability to increase your existing goals, or even set new ones.

Strong reasons create movement toward a greater life in two ways:

1. **Push** – They can push you toward your goal (earning more money).
2. **Pull** – They can pull you away from something negative (an alcohol addiction).

WHY PEOPLE AVOID ESTABLISHING REASONS

Reasons cause goals to become real. When you attach them to a goal, it moves that goal from wishful thinking to great thinking. Attaching strong reasons to support a goal causes you to tap into your emotions. However, many people are not prepared to make that kind of emotional commitment.

There are two reasons people avoid establishing strong reasons:

1. **Themselves** – They do not want to let themselves down.
2. **Others** – They do not want to let others down.

It is one thing to write down, "I want to stop smoking." It is another thing to write down, "I need to stop smoking because I do not want to develop emphysema." That is a compelling reason. Many people have goals with reasons like that, but they avoid focusing enough on their reasons. When you ignore your reasons, you will not accomplish your important goals.

People who avoid establishing strong reasons are not serious about accomplishing their goals in the first place. Many people go through the process of goal setting because it provides a temporary feeling of forward momentum. They do this repeatedly, gaining the same good feeling, but go nowhere. Strong reasons will put your goals into perspective and you into motion.

Writing your goals down allows you to look at them on paper. But, attaching strong reasons to them causes you take a closer look at yourself. Establishing your reasons will force you to be honest with yourself about your level of commitment.

By going through the process of setting goals and letting them fall by the wayside, year after year, most people get pretty good at fooling themselves. Strong reasons help you assess just how committed you are. Are you important enough to yourself, to let your reasons push you to greatness?

Establishing strong reasons will also cause you to examine how you feel about those who are close to you. For most people, it is easier to let yourself down than to let your family or friends down. So, if your goal is to stop smoking and you add a loved one as a reason, it may sound like this, "I need to stop smoking because I do not want to develop emphysema and miss out on seeing my daughter grow up." That is much more powerful. You would not let her down, would you?

THE BENEFIT OF ESTABLISHING REASONS

Establishing strong reasons not only allows you to accomplish goals, but it can also help to expand the scope of your dreams. Sometimes the reasons behind the goal are so strong, that the goal itself will become bigger than originally intended. The same reasons that caused the goal to grow will also ensure that it will be accomplished.

Imagine having the goal of building a structure that stood over 400 feet tall. Now imagine that the materials necessary to construct it weighed over 5.9 million tons. That is a pretty 'heavy' goal (sorry, I couldn't resist). Imagine further, that you had this idea over 4,500 years ago. You had no cranes or other motorized equipment. You had no computer programs. And you had no steel. You would need to have a truly compelling reason to not only set a goal like this, but to find the motivation to start it and see it through!

History has proven that if your reason is strong enough, nothing can stop you from achieving greatness. The Great Pyramid of Giza took almost twenty years to complete and required the efforts of over

100,000 men. It is the last of the Seven Wonders of the Ancient World still standing – 4,500 years later! That is a great achievement!

To the Egyptians, this was more than just a mere structure. It had a much deeper meaning. The pyramid's architectural design was so precise that each side of the pyramid is slightly concave, meaning that each face of the pyramid is indented from the corner to the midpoint of the base. But, for most of its existence, the base of the pyramid was thought to be merely a square.

In 1940, archeologists discovered that the base of the great pyramid actually formed a four-pointed star, when they photographed it aerially for the first time. This specific feature can only be seen accurately from the air, at certain times of the day. Designing and building this pyramid is amazing, especially when you consider that the Egyptian builders had no way to view it from the air and they had no technological tools to help with the design.

What would motivate people to attempt a goal of this size? The reason for building this pyramid was to create a tomb for Fourth Dynasty Egyptian Pharaoh Khufu. The pyramid was designed to have perfect alignment to the stars. This would allow their Pharaoh's spirit to rise up and travel into the heavens. Why they built it was far more important than what they built.

REASONS GIVE STRENGTH

One of my goals was to make money in the financial services industry. I needed to put food on the table and pay for our rent and utilities, but my reason was much deeper for me. With everything Gina was going through, the last thing she needed was to focus on our lack of money. The words of Gina's oncologist rang out in my head every day, "Keep her positive, it can save her life."

At this time, I was faced with many challenges and often felt depressed. My success in the financial services industry relied on my ability to per-form dynamic face-to-face presentations. In order to sell, the spotlight was constantly focused on me. I had to appear energetic and excited to my potential clients, even when I was wondering if my wife would live or die.

Unfortunately, I did not make money as fast as I had expected to. These were scary times, which did not help me to keep a positive attitude in my cancer patient at home! With no base salary to fall back on, everything was based on my personal performance. My financial goals were paramount. But, I often lacked the energy to go into the office, let alone go into the field.

If I did not write new business, I did not get paid. My challenges often seemed too overwhelming to stay focused on my goals. Luckily, I had attached very powerful reasons that motivated me to get out and accomplish those goals.

It was not the financial struggle that pushed me during this time. It was my desire to give Gina positive news every day. So I made the commitment to go into the office and book as many appointments as I could. When I returned home, Gina would wishfully ask me how many appointments I had scheduled. When appointments were set, I saw her excitement. But, when business was closed, I saw her relief.

Each night I would try to have at least two appointments. I would schedule them at 6 p.m. and 8 p.m. Sometimes, I did not get home until 11 p.m. But it did not matter because my reasons for earning money were truly strong. I was not about to give up. In fact, my reasons even motivated me enough to help overcome my own personal fear of going into the field and public speaking.

When I started thinking great, I found myself scheduling more appointments than I could physically handle myself. I began to improve my presentations and my closing skills. In fact, other agents started to request that I go on their appointments with them, to help them close the sale, or as I like to say, open new opportunities. My calendar started to get so packed that I had to send other agents out to meet with my clients. On those sales, I would split the commission with them.

This gave me the opportunity to spend more time with Gina and make money at the same time. That was a welcome relief for both of us because her condition was still very bad. Sometimes I had three scheduled appointments on the same night. By sending out other agents, I would still make 50% on each sale. In essence, I made 150% that night! I was finally making more and working less!

If I had only focused on my goals, I too, may have quit when the tough times arrived. By focusing on my strong reasons, I empowered myself to stay on track and take the remaining steps. My reasons allowed me to receive one of the fastest promotions in the company and start collecting bigger overrides on my team.

When you have important reasons powering your vehicle, you will not only get over the speed bumps, you will arrive at new opportunities.

There are two types of reasons you can attach to your goals:

1. **Positive Reasons** – These reasons will have a positive impact in your life and will provide you with the motivation you need to accomplish your goals.
2. **Negative Reasons** – These reasons will have a negative impact in your life and will create consequences for not accomplishing your goals.

Both positive reasons and negative reasons provide you with a great deal of motivation. Identifying both often works better than just focusing on one. My strong reasons have always revolved around my family. When I am pursuing my goals, I always focus on my reasons. I love to put up a picture of my strongest reasons: my family!

There is only one purpose for establishing strong reasons, and that is to empower yourself to accomplish your goals. Each of your goals will have many strong positive and negative reasons for accomplishing them. In order to achieve a greater life, you will need to focus on your deepest and most motivating factors.

STEP 2: ESTABLISH POWERFUL REASONS FOR ACCOMPLISHING YOUR GOALS

Transfer one of your most important goals from the end of Chapter 2, and list as many strong reasons that you can think of for accomplishing this goal. List your Positive Reasons and Negative Reasons.

Here are few tips to help set high expectations:

- Focus on *why* you need to accomplish this goal.
- Think about how other people will benefit from accomplishing this goal.
- Are your reasons compelling enough to move you to take action?

Here is an example of the reasons I attached to writing my first book:

Goal #1   Write a book

Reasons: To share a powerful message

                 To fulfill the dream of becoming an author

Next, attach a picture of your strongest reason(s) for accomplishing this goal. If you are striving for a greater life and the accomplishment of your goals benefits others, put up their picture.

Chapter 4

E – Expectations

Set High Expectations for Yourself!

We all have basic expectations in our lives, such as showing up on time for work, dropping the kids off at school, and paying bills. Setting *high* expectations for yourself acknowledges that your goals are important to you and that you believe in your abilities to accomplish them. These expectations will enable you to apply the right *productive pressure* to your efforts.

Many people are ready to pursue their goals. When you set high expectations, it is like jumping on a trampoline. But this process can be a fairly new experience to most people. High expectations will work hand-in-hand with your strong reasons, which in turn, work with your powerful goals.

There are two types of expectations:

Mental – these are the expectations you have placed on your thoughts (inner dialogue).

Physical – these are the expectations you have placed on your actions (outer dialogue).

In general, most people only set expectations on their actions (physical expectations). They push themselves to get to the gym, stop buying on credit, or dedicate time to writing their novel. These expectations are decisive in achieving greatness. But they work much better when they are aligned with mental expectations. Mental expectations are frequently not understood and are often underutilized. They allow you to control what kind of thoughts enter your head.

Your thoughts can either be positive or negative, but you cannot have both at the same time. The human mind will focus on the actions which are in alignment with your dominating thoughts. By keeping your thoughts positive, you can set the high expectation of, "I will not quit." Raising the bar on your own expectations is similar to applying pressure to a lump of coal. Enough pressure will produce a diamond. Apply enough *productive pressure* on your efforts and you will produce a true gem... greatness. Unlike tasks, you cannot assign someone else to fulfill your expectations.

Setting high expectations is about stepping out of your comfort zone!

THE IMPACT OF EXPECTATIONS

Setting high expectations forces you to ask significant questions pertaining to the accomplishment of your goals. These are questions that everyone who strives for greatness must answer. Their answers dictate their level of success.

What will you sacrifice to achieve a greater life? There is no such thing as something for nothing. Your goals will require that you sacrifice time, money, and/or luxuries. There is always a price for greatness. Are you willing to pay it? Only you can answer this. Only you can guarantee to pay the price required for a greater life.

Setting high expectations is like going to the gym and lifting weights for the first time. It is exciting when you get there and see all the other people working out. The sound of the music and the shiny equipment are motivating. You can start to picture the dramatic results your body will get if you stick with the program consistently.

After working out, you can be physically exhausted, but you usually feel great... until the next morning! You wake up and your muscles are sore, even the ones you did not know you had. This can be an uncomfortable feeling. Many people are so uncomfortable with feeling 'uncomfortable' that they never make it to their next workout!

Soreness (not pain) is a sign that progress is being made. The soreness eventually goes away, and the results start to show. Setting high expectations will help you achieve amazing results by getting you to step out of your comfort zone. Remember, in order to Think G.R.E.A.T., you need to think differently.

When you encounter challenges in your life, you will be better prepared to overcome them if you have high mental and physical expectations. High expectations will also separate you from the status quo crowd. People who set high expectations typically have a different confidence level. They walk and talk differently than those operating with low expectations. Having high expectations create a dynamic aura around you, one that attracts others with similar expectations for themselves.

It is important to realize that feelings such as stress, fear and worry have no physical properties. They only exist in your mind. So how do they enter your mind? Simple, you allow them in. These three mental aspects are some of the biggest enemies we have, yet they are unreal unless we allow them to exist! It takes the same energy to fill your mind with hope, excitement and passion. High mental expectations will give you the power to control your thoughts.

WHY PEOPLE AVOID SETTING EXPECTATIONS

Alexander Pope wrote, "Blessed is he who expects nothing, for he shall never be disappointed." Unfortunately, he shall never achieve greatness either. People who avoid setting expectations, are usually trying to avoid the possibility of being disappointed. The biggest downside to that way of thinking is that when you expect nothing, you usually get just that... nothing!

Setting high expectations is nothing more than putting pressure on yourself. Since most people lean toward the status quo, any added pressure in their lives, even productive pressure, can be hard to handle. You cannot go through life worried about what might go wrong. By dedicating that same energy to raising the bar, you can start to enjoy a richer, more fulfilled life. Both the good and the bad you find in life are a direct result of the expectations you set for yourself.

People who avoid setting high expectations are usually pessimistic. They find the negative in everything. Their motto is "If something can go wrong, it will go wrong." Avoidance of expectations is familiar ground to those who consider themselves 'realists' as well. Their motto is "Don't rock the boat." There is nothing wrong with being 'realistic' unless it allows you to justify not doing anything with your life.

Setting high expectations are usually reserved for those optimistic 'dreamers' who want more from life. Their motto is "If it is meant to be, it is up to me." In life, there are followers and there are leaders. When it comes to setting high expectations, whether in your personal or professional life, it tends to be done by a leader. Both pessimistic and realistic individuals tend to be followers, and more often than not, followers rarely exceed the expectations of their leaders.

Ask yourself this question about your life, "If you are only following, who is leading?" That is a scary question, but probably not as scary as the answer. Those who are not leading their own lives, rarely attempt to set expectations, much less high ones. Setting high expectations in your life is also a guarantee that your life is going to change! Some people are opposed to any type of change in their lives, even if it is a change for the better. The worst part about being afraid of change is that you can become comfortable with settling for whatever hand life deals you. And believe me, life will deal you something.

Setting high expectations changes you from *worrier* to *warrior*.

THE BENEFIT OF SETTING HIGH EXPECTATIONS

Remember, difficulties are part of life, so setting high expectations can serve as a form of preventative maintenance. They allow you to achieve greatness, even if it is in an area of your life you never imagined. Whether someone is coasting down the path of 'status quo,' or racing up the path of 'status grow,' just a single event in their life can affect everything. If you fail to set high expectations, you may not only get knocked off course, but it could destroy your life.

In 1981, a six-year-old boy was abducted from the toy department in Sears. After a sixteen-day search, his mother and father were given the horrific results of that search. John and Revé Walsh would never see their young son, Adam, alive again. He was abducted and brutally murdered.

Those were different times in our country and crimes were not as publicized as they are today. The Walsh family saw the need to change that and looked for ways to help missing and exploited children. Their efforts led to the creation of the Missing Children's Act of 1982 and the Missing Children's Act of 1984. Setting the bar even higher, they founded the Adam Walsh Child Resource Center, a non-profit organization dedicated to legislative reform.

Their story was first told when NBC aired Adam in 1983 and Adam: His Song Continues in 1986. After both programs, the network published a list of missing children which led to the recovery of 65 children. John Walsh's high expectations of bringing these criminals to justice led him to host the television show America's Most Wanted since 1988. Because of his high expectations, his goal of bringing child predators to justice expanded to include many other types of criminals. In the twenty years since the show was launched, nearly 1,000 fugitives have been caught.

John Walsh has been honored five times, by four different presidents: Ronald Reagan (twice), George H. W. Bush, Bill Clinton, and George W. Bush. He has also been honored by both the U.S. Marshals and the FBI. One of their biggest accomplishments came when John and Revé stood beside President George W. Bush as he signed the Adam Walsh Child Protection and Safety Act of 2006, which provides tougher laws on sex offenders who tend to disappear after their release from prison.

After the tragedy, John and Revé had three more children. More than 25 years passed without receiving justice in the crime against Adam, but the high expectations they set have helped thousands of others to receive their justice sooner.

HIGH EXPECTATIONS PUSH YOU HIGHER

When I was serving in the Marine Corps, I dreamt of writing and directing action movies. I spent all of my free time writing script ideas back at the barracks and I even took a pen and paper into the field when I was on deployment. In 1988, I shipped out for over three weeks and lived in a tent in the middle of the desert at the Marine base in Palm Springs.

It was the end of August and the daily temperatures were well over 110 degrees. We had no air conditioning in the tents, but that did not stop me from writing! I had set some pretty high expectations on myself to get into the entertainment industry after my tour of duty was up.

Immediately after Gulf War I ended, I was honorably discharged from active duty. A few weeks later, I started film school at Orange Coast College in Costa Mesa, California. In high school, I was not very motivated, and my grades reflected that. But I was excited about going to college and pursuing my goals. I enrolled in four film classes during my first semester.

When I received my first report card, I had to do a double-take. I had straight A's. My family and friends were as surprised as I was. There it was, staring me in the face, a 4.0 G.P.A. for my first semester. I loved the feeling so much that I set my expectations high for the next semester. I did it again. Another 4.0. My high expectations caused me to set a new goal. No longer did I just want to graduate, I wanted to graduate with a 4.0.

One year and eight months after starting college, I graduated with a 4.0 G.P.A., became the class Valedictorian, and gave the opening speech as the graduation speaker. I was accepted to the University of Southern California (USC) and attended their production program at the School of Cinematic Arts. I continued to keep my mental and physical expectations high and soon started my career in the entertainment industry. I had finally made it. I was in the career that I had been passionate about for so long.

I worked in the entertainment industry for four years before Gina was diagnosed with cancer. Our lives took a very different path and we were forced to reset more than just our goals. As I switched careers to the financial services industry, I would discover the importance of strong reasons, especially for a career I was less passionate about.

To earn money, I raised every expectation I could. In the beginning phase of any sales career, you may encounter more rejection than you anticipate. Rejection can be tough to handle, especially when you have a wife with cancer and she is awaiting your good news! At first, success was few and far between.

I learned that most sales occur after the fifth call is made to the potential client. So, I set my expectations to ten. Many co-workers gave up after the first call. But I just kept calling and eventually, would get a 'Yes.' I absolutely could not afford rejection. So I set an extremely high mental expectation of not hearing it! I changed my thinking and never heard 'No.' 'No' was merely the first two letters of 'Not yet.' They had not finished their sentence, and I knew that they would come around and eventually need my services.

You never know when life will cause you to develop new goals. The purpose of setting high expectations is to push you closer toward your goals, not push you over the edge! Even though you have 24 hours in your day, you cannot schedule 24 hours of activities. Your expectations need to be high but achievable.

MORE OR LESS?

High expectations are meant to provide you with more momentum, not cause you to lose it. If your goal is to lose weight, you most likely need to add the habit of exercising to your schedule, while simultaneously eliminating the habit of eating junk food. That's usually easier said than done. Habits are not created, nor broken overnight. If it were that easy, everyone would pursue and achieve greatness with little effort.

Getting your expectations to align with your reasons may take some time. It takes complete dedication. Habits, especially bad ones, can have a strong hold on you. You may not know how strong until you decide to eliminate them. But you absolutely can do it. Thousands already have! Focus on improving a little each day.

High Expectations fall into two categories:

1. Doing More Good Habits
2. Doing Less Bad Habits

Make the connection between your expectations and your reasons. You cannot expect to develop ten new great habits and eliminate ten bad habits the first week. If you eat fast food for lunch, reduce it to one meal for the week. As that becomes a habit, start eliminating fast food altogether. If a goal requires little effort, it is a good sign that it probably will not help you achieve a greater life.

Do not set your expectations low – you may hit them! Always set the bar high for yourself. To add to the momentum, you have created by identifying your goals and attaching strong reasons to them, let's set your High Expectations!

STEP 3: SET HIGH EXPECTATIONS FOR YOURSELF

Transfer your goal and reasons from the end of Chapter 3. Now, identify as many high *mental* expectations as you can which will help accomplish your goal.

Next, list out as many high *physical* expectations as you can which will help push you closer to this goal.

Here are few tips to help set high expectations:

- Set expectations that push you out of your comfort zone.
- Focus on being the leader of your life, not the follower.
- Identify both your good and bad habits

Here's an example of setting expectations for your goals:

Goal #1:   Write a book

Reasons: To share a powerful message

                  To fulfill the dream of becoming an author

Expectations: Allocate time every day to writing a new full page

Chapter 5

A – Actions

Take All of the Actions Necessary to Achieve a Greater Life!

"Every Marine is a rifleman." Regardless of what job we performed in the Marine Corps, we were trained extensively with our M16-A2 Assault Rifles. Once issued, our rifles were with us at all times during boot camp. Like most recruits, my goal was to qualify at the rifle range so, I could advance to the next phase of boot camp. Our drill instructors would make sure that every action we took would help us to reach that goal.

The importance of accurately firing our weapon cannot be understated. At night, before going to sleep, the entire platoon would recite the *Rifleman's Creed*. Here is the beginning of our creed:

> This is my rifle. There are many like it, but this one is mine. It is my life. I must master it as I must master my life. Without me, my rifle is useless. Without my rifle, I am useless. I must fire my rifle true. I must shoot straighter than the enemy who is trying to kill me. I must shoot him before he shoots me. I will.

My goal may have been to qualify with my rifle, but it was my reason that truly motivated me: to stay alive in combat. With a reason like that, my expectations remained high. I dedicated extra time to studying my weapon and practicing my firing techniques, like position and breathing.

Before stepping foot onto the rifle range with live ammunition, we performed precise drill movements for hours at a time. We learned how to maneuver our rifles in perfect unison, until our rifles became an extension of our bodies. Sergeant Hughes was a perfectionist at the highest level who knew the importance of the actions we would perform on the firing range. He trained us with an intensity that has carried on to other important areas of my life.

As our platoon marched to the drill field to practice our maneuvers, we understood that this was part of a much bigger picture. Sergeant Hughes ordered us to 'halt' and we took a final step, as one, and stood at attention. He slowly walked around our platoon and described, in great detail, the drill movements we would perform for the next few hours.

Before giving us the command to 'march,' he always ended with one powerful statement, "practice does not make perfect; perfect practice makes perfect." While I do not recommend striving for perfection, I do feel it is important to consistently make progress.

On the rifle range, the strict adherence to these actions would lead to the accomplishment of our goal – qualifying with our rifles. But, I would utilize this laser-focused approach and apply it to every action I take. Identifying powerful goals, establishing strong reasons, and setting high expectations has prepared me to do one thing – take action.

The difference between where you are and where you want to be, is what you do. Most people know what they need to do to accomplish their goals: exercise, eat healthier, save money, stop wasting time, etc. But they fail to take the right actions.

There is an old adage that knowledge is power. If you are going to achieve a greater life, you need to think differently. Knowledge is not power. Combining knowledge and action is power. *The GOAL Formula* will provide you with much knowledge, but you must take the actions!

ROWING YOUR BOAT

Some people confuse movement with action. Going to the gym is different than working out, but both require energy. Treading water is different than swimming, but both require energy. The difference between movement and action is distance. Movement keeps you in the same location, but actions will take you to new destinations.

Taking action is much like rowing a boat. Imagine that you are on the shore of a lake and your goals are on an island, in the middle. You step over to a small boat, floating in the water. Two dry oars are laid across the cracked wooden seat, waiting for someone to put them in the water. Getting to your goals seems simple enough. Get in the boat and row!

If it is that easy, why do so many fail to get across the lake? When most people decide to take action, to pursue their goals, they begin with the best of intentions. They start off strong, rowing with a ton of passion and excitement. But they soon find that they are simply going in circles. Most goals remain on that island in the middle of the lake, even though a great deal of energy is being exhausted rowing the boat.

Your Two Oars:

1. **Knowing** – Having the right knowledge
2. **Doing** – Combining that knowledge with the right actions

Most people row with one oar. When you take action, rowing with both oars will allow you to travel in a straight line and get to your goals faster, without wasting energy. If you gather knowledge, but never apply it, you will spin in circles. If you take action without the necessary knowledge, you will spin in circles. Either way, your goals remain stranded.

When you pursue goals, but never see results, you use a lot of energy. You can get tired, frustrated, and confused, ending up exactly where you began. When you row with both oars, you not only move in the right direction, you create more momentum. You turn your row boat into a battleship! It may take extra energy to get it going, but once you are moving forward, it can be very difficult to stop.

Rowing with both oars also allows you to take action, even when you do not feel like it. I have often had the best workouts on the days I did not feel like going to the gym. When you take the right actions, combined with the right knowledge, you immediately begin to enjoy the satisfaction of taking your life into your own hands.

Stop for a moment and reflect on what you have accomplished thus far! You took action as soon as you began marking this book up. Writing your goals, reasons, and expectations are three steps toward a greater life. How does that feel? If you are like most Great Thinkers, you must feel pretty good.

Once you have momentum, stay with it. Getting something to start moving again always takes more energy than keeping it going. A standard battleship can weigh 4,500 tons. A great amount of energy is required to get it moving at a top speed of 31 knots (about 35 mph). Now imagine trying to get it to stop! Even by taking evasive measures, it may still require 600 yards to stop. That's two full football fields.

The actions you choose to take are also similar to rowing a boat. Getting to your destination has a lot to do with what direction you move in.

Three Types of Actions:

Reverse – 'Status No'

These actions divert you away from your goal. Spending money on an expensive, high-calorie dinner will affect your goal of getting out of debt and your goal of losing weight. Even though you are moving, you are heading in the wrong direction.

Neutral – 'Status Quo'

These actions keep you in the same spot. You are exerting energy, but you are not going anywhere. Spending time watching television when you could be working on your novel will keep your boat 'docked'.

Forward – 'Status Grow'

These actions move you in the direction of your goals. Eating right, taking that college course, spending quality time with your family, or anything else you desire, can help you achieve greatness. In fact, moving forward is the only way you can.

There is only one purpose for taking action and that is to accomplish your goals. Taking *forward* action transforms your expectations into motion. Be aware of the actions you take. Remember, "perfect practice makes perfect." But consistent progress will serve you best. Only your actions will produce results.

WHY PEOPLE AVOID TAKING ACTION

Taking action requires vision. You must be able see the final result in your head. Without the vision of your completed goal, it will be difficult to act effectively. Michelangelo Buonarroti, the Italian Renaissance artist, had great vision. His vision led to his actions.

Michelangelo is known for carving the Statue of David, painting the ceiling of the Sistine Chapel, and designing St. Peter's Basilica. He visualized each masterpiece before taking any action. He is quoted as saying, "I saw the angel in the marble and I carved until I set him free."

Your goals already exist. The body you want is already there, under the body you currently have. The income you want is already there, it just has to be earned. The book you are writing already exists in your mind. You just have to put it onto paper. Those who fail to take action usually lack the vision to see their own potential to complete the goal. That's why having a big picture will help stack the deck in your favor.

Taking action also requires self-confidence. Most people are afraid to commit to the level of dedication required to accomplish their goals. Michelangelo created his masterpiece by consistently chipping away at the marble. By taking these small 'multiple' actions he moved forward until he achieved what his mind had already seen. The final statue was always there, just waiting on his actions. How many of your goals are waiting for you to start chipping away at them? Are you ready to set your goals free?

Actions will transfer your intentions into reality.

TAKING ACTION ALLOWS YOU TO INSPIRE OTHERS TO GIVE BACK

Taking the necessary actions to achieve a greater life can require a great deal of energy, especially during less than optimum circumstances. Early in Gina's treatments, friends and family visited her at our home and at the hospital. They talked, prayed, laughed, and gave her comfort. But the best visits were always from cancer survivors, usually people we did not know personally.

The amount of hope they gave her was immeasurable. Their actions inspired us to think differently about our actions. Remember, it was the visit from a stranger that helped to define my greater purpose. A single person, taking the right actions, can make a great difference. Today, Gina and I volunteer our time in the fight against cancer, through the Relay For Life. One of our goals is to bring hope to patients, caregivers, and survivors.

In 1985, a man from Tacoma, Washington, made the decision to take action and personally raise money to fight cancer. Dr. Gordy Klatt, a colorectal surgeon, wanted to help his local American Cancer Society chapter and show his support for all of his patients who had battled cancer. He wanted to accomplish his goal by doing something he enjoyed – running marathons. In May of that same year, Dr. Klatt spent 24 grueling hours circling the track at Baker Stadium at the University of Puget Sound in Tacoma.

During this first *Relay*, he enlisted the support of nearly 300 of his friends, family, and patients to watch as he ran and walked the course. Throughout the evening, they donated $25 to run or walk with Dr. Klatt for 30 minutes and help with his goal. By the end of the 24-hour period, he had run for more than 83 miles and raised $27,000 to fight cancer! While he was running the track, he began to think about how others could join him in his mission to fight cancer. He envisioned the creation of a 24-hour team event to raise even more money.

Over the next few months, Dr. Klatt formed a small committee to plan the first team relay event, known as the City of Destiny Classic 24-Hour Run Against Cancer. In 1986, Dr. Klatt enlisted the help of Pat Flynn, now known as the 'Mother of Relay', and 19 teams took part in the first team Relay. The event occurred at the historic Stadium Bowl and raised $33,000. On the track dotted with tents, something great emerged that day.

The incredible spirit behind the Relay for Life was born. More than just a fundraiser, Relay allows members of the community to participate and celebrate cancer survival. Every event begins with a Survivors Lap in which cancer survivors take a victory lap around the track. Later in the evening, a candlelight ceremony is held to honor survivors, and to remember those who have been lost to the dreadful disease.

Here are some of the amazing results that Dr. Klatt's actions helped to bring about:

- Since 1985, over 45,000 Relay events have been held in the United States.
- Since 1985, Relay for Life has raised over $3 billion – making it the largest global fund-raiser of its kind.
- In 1996, Relay for Life went international and reached 19 other countries.
- In 2008, more than 3.5 million people participated in the Relay for Life.
- In 2008, more than $409 million was raised.
- In 2008, over 500,000 cancer survivors took part in a Relay.

By taking his first step on that track in 1985, Dr. Klatt's actions have brought together millions of people for a greater purpose. It all started with the goal of raising money locally but has turned into something far greater. Each year the Relay for Life grows and continues to raise money in hopes of eliminating cancer. Currently, 1 in every 100 Americans participates in the fight against cancer through the Relay for Life!

STEP 4: TAKE ALL OF THE ACTIONS NECESSARY

Trying to accomplish goals without taking all of the necessary actions is like driving a car without all of the tires. Yes, you can get some momentum going, but it will not last long, and you will not go very far. Achieving a greater life is about doing 100% of what is required.

Transfer your goal, reasons and expectations from the end of Chapter 4. Underneath each expectation, list the actions you will need to take in order to fulfill them.

Here are few tips to help take action:

- Do not confuse gaining knowledge with taking action

- Taking small steps is better than taking no steps at all
- Take immediate action

Here's an example of identifying the necessary actions for your goals:

Goal #1:   Write a book

Reasons: To share a powerful message

                  To fulfill the dream of becoming an author

Expectations: Allocate time every day to writing a new full page

Actions: Purchase writing materials

                  Find an agent

                  Perform necessary research

                  Write for one hour before going to bed

Chapter 6

T – Tracking

Track Your Results Intensely!

Your goals are too important to just 'wing-it.' Because you, your goals, and your life mean so much, you have put a great amount of effort to get to this point. Transforming your goals into greatness is like making a fine meal. The only way to cook it is to apply the right amount of heat. Greatness rarely happens at room temperature!

You have undoubtedly started to feel the excitement of taking the right actions to accomplishing your goals. I am confident that your goals have the potential to be life-changing. Whether you need to be a better parent, help someone to beat an addiction, restart a career, or change the world, you will need a system to make sure your plan is heading in the right direction and stays on track.

This final step, which is usually the most challenging for many people, will keep you in control while on your journey to achieving a greater life. In order to measure your progress, it is crucial to track your results. By measuring the progress of your short-term goals, you will gain the valuable information needed to ensure that you are on track with your long-term goals.

Tracking your results forces you to be honest with yourself. At the end of each day, you have to answer to yourself for what you did or did not accomplish. Great Thinkers use tracking as a way to course-correct their direction as they travel to reach their goals. Implementing personal accountability is crucial, but it is without a doubt, one of the most difficult areas for people.

I believe that the first four steps will put you on course to accomplishing your goals, but if you are looking to exceed them, 'tracking' will give you the advantage. Tracking your results also creates energy and excitement, allowing you to measure your progress and increase your performance. As your performance increases, so do your odds of accomplishing your goals.

TAKING AIM

After one month in boot camp, my platoon loaded into a bus and traveled to Edson Range, located on the Marine Corps Base at Camp Pendleton. Until this point, we had not loaded a single round of ammunition into these weapons. For the next two weeks, under the close watch of our drill instructors, we would learn the strategies and techniques needed to hit the target.

Ironically, we did not receive any ammunition during our first week there. We fired the rifle, but the ammo was imaginary! We spent hours every day 'snapping in.' Our entire platoon sat in a grass field, circling a single white barrel about fifty feet from us. A few dozen targets, of different sizes and shapes were stenciled on it.

They represented the different targets we would be aiming at on the actual firing range. Day after day, we stared through our front sight post, aiming at the barrel. We practiced our breathing, exhaling slightly as we squeezed the trigger until it clicked. We adjusted our positions, lined up our sights and fired. We did this hundreds of times without real ammunition because every shot was important.

The objective of rifle training is for recruits to accurately hit the paper targets. The objective in combat is for Marines to accurately hit live targets – before they fire back! No one questioned the importance of accuracy on the rifle range. By the time we received our first live round of ammunition, we would have one week to fully qualify with our weapons. If we failed, we would be sent back, with another platoon, to start the process over. That was never a good thing!

Loading our weapons with live ammunition was quite a rush. We would be firing at targets at distances of 200, 300, and 500 yards. There were many factors to consider before firing each round:

- Positions: sitting, standing, kneeling, or prone (laying)
- Distance from the target
- Breathing techniques
- Shape of the target
- Wind adjustments – checking the velocity of the flag on the range
- Weather conditions – is it raining or foggy?
- Slow fire or rapid fire?

At the 500-yard range (the length of five football fields), the target was so small that it seemed impossible to hit. I carefully lined up my first shot and exhaled until my front sight post completely covered the target. I concentrated with the greatest intensity and slowly began to squeeze the trigger. I knew that any jolt at this distance would cause me to be way off target. I continued to squeeze the trigger until my rifle fired, sending the bullet 'down range' at 3,000 feet per second.

I lowered my rifle and squinted my eyes to see the result of my shot. The 'scoring' marker rose up, signaling the accuracy of my shot – it was a bull's-eye! It was an amazing feeling. I landed the next nine shots in almost the same spot. I was no longer just seeing the targets painted on a white barrel; I was hitting the ones on the rifle range.

I had only been firing live ammunition for one week, but I was able to consistently hit the target because we were taught to track each shot. To track and course-correct our progress, we were issued a Rifle Marksmanship Data Book. The data book functioned as our daily journal and allowed us to track each shot we fired on the range.

By properly using our data books, we mastered the marksmanship techniques that week, qualified with our rifles, and moved onto the next phase. Keep in mind that most recruits had never fired a weapon before. Tracking our results, allowed us to hit the target – every time.

In order to fire our weapons accurately, we documented our actions. We tracked our position, our aiming, and other basic fundamentals. Tracking also allowed us to compensate for other variables, such as wind and weather. Without using our data book to track our results, we would have missed out on the valuable information it generated about our performance.

The data book is so critical for success that the Marine Corps describes its use in the *Marine Corps Reference Publication (MCRP) 3-01A, Rifle Marksmanship*, as follows:

> *Of all the tools that assist the Marine in firing accurately and consistently, the data book, if properly used, is the most valuable asset. It contains a complete record of every shot fired and the weather conditions and their effects on shooting. When used properly, it will assist the Marine in establishing and maintaining a battlesight zero (BZO).*

By analyzing the information that we tracked, our drill instructors could identify weaknesses and assist us with techniques to correct and improve our shooting performance. Firing my weapon accurately could mean the difference between life and death, so I not only took detailed notes in my data book; I followed the guidance of my drill instructors to the 'T.'

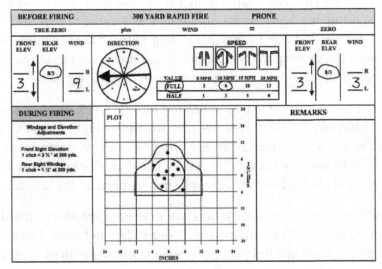

© USMC, Marine Corps Reference Publication (MCRP) 3-01A

*Example of a Rifle Marksmanship Data Book page from the Marine Corps rifle range

If your goals are important enough, you will take the time to write down your 'data' and review it to find ways to correct and improve your performance. In boot camp, our drill instructors used the word 'perfection' to emphasize the importance of the exactness of our drill movements. Perfection does not exist, and it is a waste of your time chasing it. Trying to perfectly accomplish your goals will only drain your energy and leave you disappointed.

The tracking step is all about making advances in your life, not chasing perfection. Your journey is about becoming better, becoming greater than you were when you started. To effectively track your results, I have created The G.P.S. (Goal Planning Strategy), which you will learn about in Chapter 13. All of the steps you have completed up to this point have helped to prepare you to design your G.P.S. for a successful *90 Day Run*, which we'll discuss in Chapter 8.

WHY PEOPLE AVOID TRACKING

People who track their results discuss their progress; people who fail to track their results discuss their problems. Many people avoid tracking like Superman avoids Kryptonite. They learn to deny responsibility for their own actions.

We see so many examples around us of poor accountability. Just turn on the news and you will be inundated with stories of corporate executives who squander money, of people driving under the influence of alcohol or of someone who is committing crimes against children. They all have one thing in common – they have convincing alibis, at least for themselves.

Often in the workplace, you can observe co-workers avoiding responsibility. Most use the popular saying, "It's not my job." When it comes to achieving a greater life, it is your job! You must take responsibility for all of your actions. People who do not practice accountability tend to make excuses and point fingers at others. They seem to master complaining and turn it into an art form. They are so good at it, that others usually join in. Complainers settle for less – Great Thinkers never settle!

People also avoid tracking because they associate it with being blamed for something. At work, most people, who perform well for the company, are only spoken to when they make mistakes. Managers tend to track only the bad things. It is no surprise that people avoid keeping track of their results. But, tracking is a great tool and you have to start viewing it as such – all Great Thinkers do!

You cannot be afraid of being in the spotlight. When you shine it on yourself, through tracking, it creates just the right amount of heat to force you to take action. That heat will decrease your chances for failure and increase your chances for greatness. Being in the spotlight will cause you to move toward your goals like never before!

THE IMPACT OF PERSONAL ACCOUNTABILITY

During Gina's treatments and recovery, I tried to be the best caregiver possible. I dedicated myself to taking care of my wife and providing for our family. But a sad reality caught up with me. I realized that I had stopped taking care of myself. I no longer exercised and ate a lot of fast food, usually on the go. It was during this time that I had gained over 40 pounds.

It would have been easy for me to blame our circumstances for my weight gain. I certainly had many valid excuses, if I had chosen to use them. Instead of wasting time by focusing on my excuses, I took full responsibility and determined how much total weight I needed to lose. I broke the goal of 16 pounds into smaller, weekly goals of 2 pounds per week.

I used the tracking step to stay on course and asked a good friend to help me monitor my weight loss. I knew the power of tracking my actions, so I raised the bar and gave him an incentive to help me track my results. Each week, I gave him an envelope containing $100 of my money! If I hit my goal for the week, I got my envelope back. If I failed, the money was his.

I discovered that my friend was tracking my results closely. I was determined not to give up that envelope. At the end of 90 days, I had exceeded my goal by losing 42 pounds! When you track your results, you accomplish your goals!

Tracking requires discipline, which in turn, builds integrity. Discipline is staying on course, even when no one is watching you. Integrity is doing things the right way, even when there is an easier way. When you channel both discipline and integrity into the tracking of your results, greatness soon follows.

It is always tempting to take the easy road, and that is the direction most people opt for. Even easier than that, is to wait until tomorrow to get something done. Procrastination is a dream-killer. Tracking your progress will help eliminate procrastination and will force you to continually take action!

Tracking takes a high level of personal accountability. Personal accountability will elevate the tracking of your results to an entirely new level, by making sure you are tracking 'you,' more than just tracking your results. There is a big difference between saying, "The goal has not been accomplished" and saying, "I have not accomplished my goal." This level of accountability will make you take ownership of your actions, or inactions!

Accountability, or the lack of it, got you to where you are today, and it will also get you to where you want to go. We do not always have a choice of the type of events that happen in our lives, but we always have a choice in how we respond to them. Being accountable will change your perception. You will stop seeing yourself as being formed by the past and start seeing yourself as being shaped by today.

STARTING OVER

I was still passionate about the entertainment industry, but I had been out of it for over four years. In any technical field, a lot can change in a short period of time. I revised my résumé and started to search online for any job opportunities in this field. There were many positions available, but this would require me to brush up on my technical skills. One job posting in particular caught my attention. It was for a scheduler position at a post-production company.

It was an entry-level position for a company based in Santa Monica, California. They specialized in making copies of all tape formats for movie studios, television networks, and production companies. I knew I had much more to offer, but I also understood that I had to get my foot in the door. During my first interview, all the years of thinking great in the financial services industry were about to pay off.

I met with the owner of the company and we immediately started talking about goals. The conversation led into passion, team work, and growth. He was at a stage in his business where he was ready to take his company to a new level. He was ready for greatness and I was prepared for it! After 20 minutes, I was hired.

I started my new job the next day, with much enthusiasm. I quickly learned everything to get myself up to speed and frequently met with the owner to discuss his goals for the company. His long-term goal was to increase the corporate sales numbers by at least 50%. I took that long-term goal and broke it into smaller, short-term goals, tracking every possible action you could imagine.

We tracked our phone calls, our customer visits, and the number of facility tours we conducted. But most importantly, we carefully tracked our results, our sales numbers. Our sales team met twice a day and discussed each area being tracked. Relentlessly tracking our results helped us to determine our strengths, which we built upon, and it allowed us to identify our weaknesses, which we course-corrected.

We listed our goals on a big dry-erase board and updated our results every day, for everyone to see. To further increase our motivation, I invited several of our higher-level department leaders into our daily sales meetings, and we shared our sales goals with them. Their departments processed the orders we brought in, so they were a critical part of our team. To increase our results, I used the 'envelope' technique I had used to lose weight. We announced a cash bonus, which would be paid out daily as we met our projected sales goals. This was paid out to the sales team as well as the department leaders.

Immediately, those who were never interested in 'sales,' were now interested in tracking our results! But what really enhanced the company's tracking was creating a separate override for the department leaders only. Every month, they received a bonus check for each order that was completed correctly and delivered on time. Because we averaged over 1,000 orders per month, I soon noticed that our department leaders became more focused on tracking than our sales team!

Tracking enabled us to get things done right the first time. We not only accomplished our sales goals, but we exceeded the original long-term goal by 15%. Accomplishing that goal opened the door to many other opportunities. We improved morale, increased customer satisfaction, developed new clients, and watched our team members accomplish their personal goals as well. When I first announced the idea of tracking our results, the entire team was less than thrilled. As our numbers grew, they not only became true believers, they became obsessed on it.

STEP 5: TRACK YOUR RESULTS INTENSELY

There is only one purpose for tracking your results and that is to improve your performance. Tracking requires dedication and focus because many of your actions will need to be repeated consistently to accomplish your goals.

Tracking your results also involves setting the timelines you will follow. When you are writing your book, you have to track how much you write on a daily basis, especially if your expectation is to write daily. If your goal is to lose weight, it is best to step on the scale every week rather than every day, but you can track your results to lose the weight on a daily basis, by tracking your actions, such as going to the gym, monitoring your portions, and eating at specific times of the day.

Transfer your goal, reasons, expectations, and actions from the end of Chapter 5. Underneath each action, list your plan for tracking your results.

Here are few tips to help track results:

- Set specific timelines for the completion of each action.
- You may need to course-correct along the way.
- Be honest with yourself about your true performance.

Here's an example of tracking your results:

Goal #1:   Write a book

Reasons: To share a powerful message

To fulfill the dream of becoming an author

Expectations: Allocate time every day to writing a new full page

Actions: Purchase writing materials

Find an agent

Perform necessary research

Write for one hour before going to bed

Tracking: Purchase writing materials

COMPLETED

Find an agent

IN PROGRESS

COMPLETION DATE IS AUG 3

Perform necessary research

50% COMPLETE

COMPLETION DATE IS SEP 1

Write for one hour before going to bed

Mon – 1.00 hr

Tue – 0.75 mins (need to make up the difference)

Wed – 1.00 hr

Thu – 1.25 hrs (compensated for Tues)

GREAT EXERCISES

My Definition of Greatness

Create your definition of greatness by writing down what you would consider to be life-changing. Come back and enhance it as you continue reading and doing more exercises.

EXAMPLE:

By accomplishing the goal of building a sizeable retirement fund, I will achieve greatness by having the peace of mind that, when I retire, I will never have to work again!

Your Greater Purpose

When people define their greater purpose and they act in accordance with it, they are more likely to accomplish their goals. Why are you here? Take some time to think about what your greater purpose is. Write out what you are most passionate about.

EXAMPLE:

I am passionate about my family and friends and I feel that my greater purpose is to help others to achieve greatness in their lives.

Part II

Time Mastery

Part II

Time Mastery

Control Your Time, Control Your Life!

Do you control your day or does your day control you? The average person misses opportunities to accomplish their goals because they do not understand how to take charge of their time. Time is a unique commodity. It is intangible. You cannot touch it, see it, or hear it. But to achieve a greater life, you must command it. Time is the second element in *The GOAL Formula.*

Most people treat time as a physical resource. They focus on how they can better spend it or more effectively save it, while others talk about running out of it or never having enough of it. "If only I had more time," is the most common excuse I hear from people who have failed to accomplish an important goal.

The reality is that we all have the same amount of time to apply toward our goals each day. Your results, both personal and professional, are always based on how well you control your time. But, how do you handle something that has no physical properties? You schedule it!

Ultimately, you have complete control of your life. Most people can successfully take the necessary steps to accomplishing their goals as long as nothing unexpected interferes. But, that is usually not the case. We all experience unforeseen difficulties that can get us off track. Scheduling your time will not only allow you to navigate through challenging circumstances, but it will guarantee that you take the steps toward your goals and enable you to accomplish more than you expected.

RISE AND SHINE

Boot camp started at 5:30 am to the sound of reveille blaring across the base. For 16 hours, every day, we took the steps to become Marines. Every task, assignment, and project we tackled was meticulously scheduled into our day. Every activity may have been mapped out, but our drill instructors did not make it easy for us. They shouted orders, barked commands, and expressed their thoughts about our performance, with words I cannot use here. But, I think you get the picture.

A typical day consisted of classroom training, practicing drill movements, preparing for uniform inspections, exercising, negotiating obstacle courses, running for miles, and being punished with endless amounts of push-ups. At night, we welcomed the sound of taps, signaling the end of our day.

Boot camp was tough, but we adapted to our daily, recurring tasks. Following our schedule was important to our success. But when unexpected circumstances presented themselves, we would rely on the detailed allocation of our time to help us stay on course with our goal. Additional challenges were constantly added to our schedule, making it more difficult to take each step to graduation.

They included rappelling from a thirty-foot tower, treading water in full combat gear, learning to survive in the field during any weather condition, and reporting in for mess hall duty at 4 am. No matter what we encountered, we were still responsible for completing our schedule of activities.

One survival skill in particular made it extremely difficult to stay focused on our other assignments. During field training, our platoon was deployed to the mountains of Camp Pendleton for one week. We slept under the stars and lived out of our backpacks. We marched for hours at a time, set up camp, practiced firing different weapons, and performed combat maneuvers. Of course, it happened to be during the rainy season!

One morning, we watched the sun rise as we approached a tent in the middle of nowhere. It was time to qualify with our gas masks. Yeah, that was a fun one. To qualify, we needed to successfully 'don and clear' our masks. Essentially, we would be removing our masks, then putting them back on, with an air – tight seal. That sounds simple enough. But, it wasn't.

The exercise would be performed in a tent filled with gas. It was the same type of chemical used by police departments for riot control. The gas would slightly burn any exposed skin, so we knew it would be painful if it made contact with our eyes. The thought of breathing it was an entirely different level of fear.

Cautiously, we entered the tent. It was so quiet, you could hear a pin drop, even with our masks on. The drill instructors had used such a large amount of gas that you could see layers of it hovering throughout. We stood in formation, nervously awaiting our first command. Breaking the silence, a drill instructor loudly ordered, "Remove your masks!" We closed our eyes, held our breath and took off our masks.

We anxiously waited for the order to 'don and clear.' It seemed like they waited until the last possible second. My lungs were screaming for air and my eyes were closed tight. Just before I needed to inhale, we were instructed to 'don and clear.' We quickly put our masks back on, formed a tight seal around our face, and exhaled to force the gas out of the mask. If we performed it correctly, we would not get any in our eyes or lungs. If we failed, we would know it immediately.

With our masks securely on, we slowly opened our eyes and took a small breath. We did it. What a great accomplishment! It was not as bad as we thought. The fear of the gas chamber was just that – fear! I was excited to step out of that tent and take a breath of fresh mountain air. But, this was Marine Corps boot camp. To help us experience the full impact of the gas, our drill instructors made us perform one final task.

In a single-file line, we stepped up to them. I was about five recruits back, so I had plenty of time to watch what was in store for me. It seemed like an eternity, but it was quickly my turn. I stepped up and locked my eyes on the top of my drill instructor's gas mask. We were not allowed to make direct eye contact with them. He sternly announced my direct order, "Take that mask off!" I had done it before, so I knew I could do it again.

I closed my eyes, took another deep breath, and removed my mask. The next order came, but it was not 'don and clear.' It was 'open your eyes!' Reluctantly, I opened them up. The burning sensation was instantaneous. My eyes watered up as I stood at attention. Unfortunately, I knew what was next.

He waited a moment, then ordered me to state my fifth general order. I managed to get some of it out with the remaining air in my lungs. "Sir, the recruit's fifth general order is to not quit my post until..." That was about it. I took the dreaded breath and the gas filled my lungs. I could not breathe. It felt like my body was shutting down. I began to cough violently. I felt like I was going to vomit. I felt like I was dying.

My drill instructor gave one last order, "Get the @#*! out of my tent!" I hurried out of the tent and followed my instructions to recover. Slowly, I regained the ability to breathe and regrouped with the other members of my platoon. It was only 8 am. We still had a full day ahead of us, packed with more tasks. There were no showers in the field, so we completed the rest of our day wearing camouflage uniforms covered in gas. But, we stayed on schedule.

Have you ever had something happen in your life that caused you to forget about everything else you had planned for the day? When your goals are important, schedule your time. Without the foundation of a daily schedule, it is easy to lose track of time, get off track, and fail to accomplish your goals.

In boot camp, I would have been unable to complete the steps to become a Marine without a regimented schedule. As a civilian, I have come to rely on the foundation of Time Mastery to help me accomplish my personal and professional goals.

To successfully control your time, utilize the three components of Time Mastery:

1. **Schedule Your Day**
2. **Connect Your Days**
3. **Organize Your Next 90 Days**

More than likely, you will not have a group of drill instructors to help you master your time, although it would certainly keep you on track! Take advantage of the same basic components used to transform civilians into Marines, in a short period of time, and transform your goals into accomplishments.

Chapter 7

Schedule Your Day

You cannot recapture yesterday, and tomorrow never comes.
All you have is today!

Everyone has the same amount of time each day to work with. Both in-shape and out-of-shape people have 24 hours a day. Both wealthy and poor people have seven days a week. Both winners and losers have twelve months per year. Greatness is achieved by those who schedule their day, every day. But, what is time? What causes it? Why does it slow in gravity? Why does it slow in motion? Is it a dimension?

Many of the greatest thinkers in history have pondered questions about time. People have searched for answers about the meaning of time since the beginning of... well, time. Aristotle suggested that time may actually be motion. In his 1952 book, Relativity, Einstein proclaimed that past, present, and future times exist simultaneously.

My intention is not to explain the deep philosophical interpretations of time. Instead, I want to share with you the techniques and strategies I have used to control a small block of time – my day. Although the concept of time will likely be discussed for centuries, there are two constants about time.

1. We all have the same amount to work with – each day.
2. We cannot recapture lost time.

Once the day is gone, it is gone. It does not matter how great someone is, no one can accomplish anything yesterday. Most people intend to accomplish their goals 'someday.' The only problem is that 'someday' never comes, it just does not exist. Check your calendar; it is not there. Not this week, next month, or the next year. All you have is today.

How you schedule your day will determine your level of success. In boot camp, each recruit is given the same amount of time to complete specific tasks. Each day is scheduled to provide us with the optimum amount of success. Putting together your big picture involves scheduling time each day to dedicate to your goals. If there is one thing to remember after reading this book, it is this: greatness takes time.

Each day your schedule is comprised of the same amount of time: 24 hours, 1,440 minutes, 86,400 seconds. While you cannot squeeze more time out of a day, you can squeeze more achievements into it by scheduling your actions. How you perceive time will determine how effectively you utilize it.

Three ways to optimize your time:

1. **Waste it** – nothing happens
2. **Spend it** – something happens
3. **Invest it** – greatness happens

Unfortunately, most people tend to waste time, rather than invest it. When Gina was diagnosed with cancer, we started to look at time much differently. When you do not know how much time you have left, every minute counts! We stopped focusing on trivial things and started to devote our time to things that mattered. Our life may have been chaotic, but our goals were still important to us. We improved our relationship with time and scheduled each day with much care, not knowing when the next challenge was coming.

YOUR RELATIONSHIP WITH TIME

Everyone has a unique way of relating to time. How you choose to view time (yes, you have a choice) will have a direct impact on your ability to schedule it in a way that aligns with your big picture.

There are three different ways to view time:

1. **Past** – Learn from the past, but do not live in it!
2. **Future** – Plan for the future, but do not wait for it!
3. **Present** – Schedule it, so you can control it!

PAST – People who live in the past tend to miss out on opportunities because they tend to focus on the failures that happened the last time they tried to accomplish something. They concentrate on people who have wronged them in the past instead of focusing on people who can help them now.

FUTURE – People who live in anticipation of the future tend to miss out on opportunities because they are always looking for a better time to arrive. They tend to over-plan, over-analyze, and under-act. They are masters of procrastination but have convinced themselves that it is for good reason. They tend to surround themselves with people who are looking for the greener grass on the other side, rather than the people who water the grass on the side they are already standing on.

PRESENT – I have saved the best for last! People who operate in the present tend to capture opportunities because they are looking for a way to move forward – right now! They tend to work with people who are also striving for a greater life, increasing their opportunity to achieve it.

YOU CAN DO A LOT WITH A LITTLE

How do you eat an elephant? While eating an elephant may not be one of your goals, it is possible if you do it one bite at a time. Even short-term goals may seem too big to tackle, when life presents obstacles. Scheduling your day allows you to keep taking the necessary 'bites' out of your goals.

Successful people guard their schedules as if their life depends on it. In fact, their 'greater life' does. As a Branch Office Manager in the financial services industry, I observed successful sales associates, and those who wanted to be successful. The difference? Their schedules.

Accomplishing sales goals was all about closing more deals. Closing more deals was all about giving more presentations. Giving more presentations was all about scheduling more appointments. Our main objective was to fill up our calendars with as many client meetings as possible, increasing our chances for success.

The great sales associates ensured that their most critical activities were scheduled during peak hours, and they did everything in their power to make sure that those well-defined blocks of time were never interrupted. To schedule more appointments, we maximized our 'Phone Zone' each morning. Much thought and time was invested in whom we called and what we expected our outcome to be.

Scheduling the actions required to accomplish your goals is much more than just penciling in a time slot in your calendar. When you take action, it is important to be fully present in the moment. Be laser-focused on what you are doing. Avoid scheduling conflicting activities. Lifting weights and reading a book are not possible at the same time, and for good reason! Even riding a stationary bike and reading do not work well together.

Your best workouts occur when you are in the zone and focused on what you are doing. You will also retain more of what you read when you are not distracted by everything else going on in the gym. Multi-tasking can be beneficial, but also has certain risks. Michelangelo did not paint the Sistine Chapel while he was trying to carve the Statue of David.

There is an old saying that states, "If you chase two rabbits, both will get away." I prefer to give myself the gift of uninterrupted time for my actions. You should too. You deserve it, and your results will reflect it. You can, however, immediately improve your efficiency by combining non-conflicting actions. You can listen to books on tape, or CD, while you are commuting to work. This is an effective way to maximize valuable time that would have been otherwise wasted!

PLAN YOUR DAY THE NIGHT BEFORE

Scheduling your day after it has already begun is like cramming for a test ten minutes before you take it. It may help somewhat, but not as much as if you had prepared for it the night before, with plenty of time to let it sink into your head. Imagine how empowered you would feel, and how much you would accomplish, if you mapped out all of your activities the night before, or perhaps the week before.

By planning out my day the night before, I have accomplished sales goals in the financial services industry as well as the entertainment industry. I never created my 'call list' on the same morning I made the calls. I put my list together well in advance, which prepared me to not only make the calls, but also stick to my schedule.

When I started the journey to lose weight, I spent the first three weeks focusing on my diet. I scheduled each meal in my calendar and ate at the same time every day. I cut out soda, minimized my bread intake, and drastically reduced the amount of fast food I ate. I experienced weight loss, but I knew I would increase my ability to hit my goal by introducing weight-training and cardiovascular exercise to my routine.

I started to work out at home, slowly building up my own gym. During the first week, I exercised specific body parts. I made note of the equipment and the amount of weight I used, after I performed each exercise. The next week, I used the same list and performed the exact routine. The difference this time, was that it was now a schedule. It was on paper. The exercises, weights, sets, and repetitions were all spelled out in front of me.

I felt more empowered doing the exercises and experienced a stronger sense of accomplishment as I marked them off. For my third week, I actually prepared a slightly new routine. But this time, the night before I exercised. I analyzed my performance and made increases to the weight I would be lifting. I was more focused during my third week and noticed that I looked forward to each routine, even 'leg' day!

Planning your next day before you go to sleep allows you to decide when the optimum times are to complete specific duties. The technique of planning out your day the night before, gives you an edge for hitting all of the goals you are striving for.

The advantage of scheduling your day in advance is that your subconscious mind has all night to think about the items you have laid out for the following day. Your mind will think of other ways to accomplish things. It is like having an extra person focusing on your goals while you are sleeping! How many times have you ever wished that you had someone to take a few steps for you? By planning the night before, you now have that.

WHAT ARE YOU WAITING FOR?

People always seem to be waiting for the right time to do something. Procrastination is a goal-killer.

- Don't wait until you have a heart attack to improve your health.
- Don't wait until you cannot retire to focus on your finances.
- Don't wait until you lose your spouse to add a spark to your marriage.
- Don't wait until your children leave the house to build a strong relationship with them.
- Don't wait until your life is almost over to start enjoying the time you have.
- Don't wait until you miss what life has to offer, when you can accomplish your goals now!

Enhance the value of your time by increasing your pace. A well-defined schedule will let your zest for life reflect in your daily activities. Schedule your day and tackle everything with energy and excitement. Now is the time for a great life! Now is the time for you to *Think GREAT*!

How would each of your days start to look if you scheduled them with a purpose? Now, imagine scheduling your activities in advance. You should be able to imagine achieving a greater life at this point.

Now, imagine connecting 90 of these days together!

Chapter 8

Connect Your Days

Use a Well-Defined Block of Time!

Rome was not built in a day, but each day was optimized to achieve their objective. Historians estimate that it took centuries of dedicated growth to reach their full potential. Like Rome, the completion of your goals will be based on consistent, scheduled activities taken on a daily basis. I have always focused on accomplishing my short-term goals in a series of well-structured days – 90 of them. I call it my *90 Day Run*. For my long-term goals, I connect multiple *90 Day Runs*.

Many of us have started personal growth programs, designed to improve certain aspects of our lives. The problem is that we usually start off strong but fail to finish. We come out of the gates excited about the new direction we are headed in and anxious to achieve great results. We successfully take the steps to our goals, for a while. But we often lose steam before accomplishing them.

Why do many of us fail to complete programs which are specifically designed to make our lives better? We fail because we do not optimize a defined block of time to operate in. People have an amazing ability to stay laser-focused and develop positive trends in their lives during a well-structured 90-day period of time. They can push themselves and accomplish goals that are life-changing.

Why 90 days? The reason for a 90-day program is that it provides the time and structure that have been proven to work. Like boot camp, your *90 Day Run* will allow you to schedule each day with goal-oriented activities, making you more efficient and effective. You will set short-terms goals, track your results and put yourself on course to accomplishing your long-term goals. Great things can happen in 90 days.

In boot camp, each of our 90 days was meticulously scheduled, flawlessly executed, and intensely tracked. But there is a big difference between boot camp and real life. As raw recruits, we lived in the barracks and functioned as a platoon. We trained together, day in and day out, focusing on the power of teamwork to help us stay on track. We were surrounded by drill instructors who were committed to our mission. Boot camp was a completely contained and regimented environment to support our actions.

Real life does not come with a perfect bubble, enveloping you and your goals. Nor does it provide you with drill instructors to monitor and course-correct your actions, guaranteeing your success. It is up to you to create the environment that will serve you best. By connecting 90 well-planned days, you can achieve a high level of success.

It is time to go on a *90 Day Run* and accomplish your goals. The following techniques and strategies were used in boot camp to motivate us, inspire us, and help us to complete our training. You can implement them in your *90 Day Run*.

CHANGING YOUR PATTERNS AND HABITS

Your current patterns of behavior and habits have brought you to where you are today or have kept you from getting where you want to be. During your *90 Day Run*, you will be launching new behaviors to help you achieve the life you want. Simultaneously, you will eliminate old patterns and habits which have prevented you from moving toward your big picture. Bad patterns and ingrained habits can be an anchor to your boat. Anchors are important, and they serve a purpose, but not when you are trying to set sail!

The first three weeks of your *90 Day Run* will be the most challenging but are very important. I have found that when people follow a new pattern in their life for three consecutive weeks, it will become a new habit. And when people stop a pattern for three weeks, they can also eliminate a habit. Your ability to stay focused during these three weeks will be critical to your success.

The Marines have a deep-rooted understanding of this principle. Boot camp is divided into three phases, each designed to effectively shape young recruits. The first few weeks of Phase 1 are specifically designed to break their civilian habits and prepare them for their new 'Marine' habits. Civilian thoughts and behavior are considered to be detrimental to training. They are eliminated during this period by intense physical training, strict discipline, new routines, and heavy instruction. And a few harsh words!

Recruits are instilled with the mental and physical discipline needed to perform under stressful situations, especially those encountered in combat. They are deliberately put into a state of constant disorientation. The purpose is to psychologically break them down, so they can successfully complete the process of becoming a United States Marine, and simultaneously be able to perform under the toughest mental and physical situations.

By the end of Phase 1, recruits have developed new habits. They can march, respond to orders, think appropriately, and perform the physical challenges thrown at them. Those who successfully eliminate their old habits and properly adopt their new ones move onto Phase 2. Those who cannot, get to repeat Phase 1. Talk about motivation. No one wanted to stay in boot camp past the 90 days, but some did.

You will not be required to shave your head or do push-ups on your *90 Day Run*, but you will be encouraged to change your patterns and habits to enable you to better support your efforts. Unlike other programs, the *90 Day Run* gives you the foundation and support you need.

Remember, when I was striving to lose weight, it took me three weeks to get adjusted to my work out. As exercising became a habit, I was able to take my routine, performance, and results to a new level. Every goal will require you to take new, unique actions. Give yourself time to adjust to them. Most people quit as soon as they feel the first hint of discomfort.

3 STAGES TO YOUR NEW ACTIONS

When greatness occurs, it is as natural as breathing – the actions often go unnoticed! Getting to that point requires practice. Being 'natural' with your new actions is a rewarding accomplishment, but the steps to get there can feel quite different at first. These feelings can be both physically and emotionally challenging. You have to adjust and adapt to any new actions.

During your *90 Day Run*, you will be more aware of the thoughts you allow to occupy your mind. Most people do not focus on this in their day-to-day lives. This is a critical reason why they do not achieve a greater life. Gina's oncologist encouraged me to focus on the thoughts filling her mind. Her life depended on it, so I stayed with it until it became natural.

At first, staying positive was a bit awkward, especially during the most challenging times. It was tough to put a positive spin on receiving chemotherapy, particularly on her seventh cycle. But I refused to give up. Eventually, it became so natural that I started helping other people to think positively. It finally helped me to define my greater purpose, launch the Think GREAT company, and teach many people how to stay on course to accomplishing their goals.

The same can be said about the actions you will take on your *90 Day Run*. Allow yourself the time required to feel natural. Understanding the three stages to your new actions will help you to get to your destination, much faster.

The three stages to your new actions:

1. **Awkward** – The initial steps of all new actions will feel awkward at first. Going to the gym every day may not agree with your muscles even though it agrees with your goals. But, most people quit when they feel awkward. *When you feel awkward, remind yourself that you are on track.*

2. **Mechanical** – Staying consistent with your actions will eliminate the awkward feelings and you will have an easier time taking your 'steps.' You will become very good at taking the repetitious actions needed to achieve a greater life. But, many people still give up when

they do not see results fast enough. *When you feel mechanical, remind yourself that you are almost there.*

3. **Natural** – At this stage, you are not only taking the necessary steps to achieve greatness, you are able to concentrate more fully on your goals. You can fine-tune your actions to enhance your results. This stage is critical because you are so close to accomplishing your goal. But, some people miss their goal because they expect it to happen at this stage. *When you feel natural, do not get over-confident, get more focused and guarantee that you get there.*

It is perfectly normal for your new actions to initially seem out of place during your *90 Day Run*. Most people feel this way in the beginning. Do not get discouraged during any one of these stages. This is the process of turning your actions into positive habits. Just know what stage you are in and focus on getting to the next level.

REWARDS AND PENALTIES

For programs to be truly successful, they must have powerful forms of incentives to motivate the accomplishment of the goal. Rewards and penalties function together as your 'incentives.' You must have the proper incentive to do something or not to do something. People do things for one of two reasons: gain pleasure (rewards) or avoid pain (penalties).

1. **Rewards** – For taking steps toward greatness – new patterns and habits
2. **Penalties** – For taking steps away from greatness – old patterns and habits

As a young recruit, I experienced many incentives. For some reason, I seem to remember more of the penalties than the rewards. But I did make it out as a Marine. Just like boot camp, you will need to establish rewards and penalties during your *90 Day Run*.

Some businesses and organizations use 'rewards and penalties' in their construction contracts. As an incentive, the contractor will receive a bonus (reward) if the construction is completed ahead of schedule. If, however, the construction is completed behind schedule, the contractor may have to repay (penalty) money to the business or organization. No one likes to give money back, so I would say it is safe to assume that these incentives keep things on track.

You can structure your incentives to best serve your needs. Whether you set up more rewards or more penalties, the choice is yours. But, set them up in a way that will keep you motivated to move forward. Your rewards should always be linked to your goals. In boot camp, a reward may have been a few extra minutes on Sunday to write a letter. Since we went 12 weeks without seeing or speaking to our family and friends, any extra time to write a letter was golden!

Let's say your goal is to lose weight. If you lose five pounds, do not reward yourself with a banana split; reward yourself with a new outfit. Choosing the appropriate rewards can provide just the right amount of motivation you need to accomplish a goal!

I have found that penalties can usually be a bigger motivator than rewards. Maybe that is why I cannot remember many rewards in boot camp. One of our penalties was intense calisthenics in a dirt field. Any time our platoon or one of its members messed up, we were sent to the 'dirt.' We must have made many mistakes, because I remember spending a lot of time there. The 'dirt' was just that, a big dirt field where we would do endless amounts of push-ups, sit-ups, mountain-climbers, jumping jacks, leg lifts, etc. We did the exercises, over and over, until the drill instructors felt we had learned our lesson.

TIMELINES

Another powerful component of your *90 Day Run* will be the timelines you set. Let's not use the word 'deadlines.' Instead bring 'life' to your *90 Day Run* by setting timelines! Having a timeline forces you to accomplish what you planned. People have a tendency to pull off miracles when timelines are met.

Have you ever noticed how much someone accomplishes at work when their review has been scheduled, or how much they can get done before leaving on vacation? When I asked Gina to marry me, I was amazed at how much she accomplished in planning our wedding, once we set the date. When I first popped the question, we decided that we would marry in a year or two.

As we talked about the wedding, I mentioned to Gina that I would love to get married on Halloween. She immediately checked her calendar and saw that the next Halloween to fall on a Saturday was in six months! We were married six months later!

Important goals, which have timelines, get accomplished. On the second day of boot camp, our platoon attended a briefing on basic training. I cannot remember everything they told us, but there was one thing I will never forget. At the end of the meeting, one of the instructors informed us that we would graduate on November 13, 1987. That was, of course, if we passed every phase. The timeline for graduation became my dominant thought.

Around that same time, we were each issued a thick handbook. It provided us with information on everything about being a Marine. It detailed the steps involved in applying a tourniquet to a wounded Marine, firing our rifles, and surviving in the field. It even provided instructions for properly folding our underwear for inspection! We used that book every day during recruit training.

One night, I sat up in my bunk, and by flashlight, wrote the timeline, "Nov. 13, 1987" on each page of that handbook. I stared at that date until it became a reality. On November 13, 1987, I graduated from Marine Corps boot camp – 90 days after I started! Do not leave your goals to chance. Assign timelines to every goal you want to accomplish and every action you need to take.

There is one final difference between boot camp and your *90 Day Run*. Boot camp was not fun, but your *90 Day Run* should be. Enjoy the process of reaching new levels in your life. The next 90 days are coming. What will you do with them?

Chapter 9

Optimize Your Next 90 Days

Choose the Right Vehicle for Your Journey!

In 1991, I was honorably discharged from the Marine Corps after four years of service. I attended college and pursued my goal of becoming a filmmaker. Each semester, I had a combination of classes, ranging from cinematography to editing. To my surprise, I discovered that I enjoyed writing my own scripts. The creative process of transforming my ideas into screenplays caused me to enroll in more writing courses.

I met other students who had the goal of becoming writers. Some of them wanted to write children's books, while others wanted to write novels, plays, or television scripts. They were all passionate about writing the stories that were floating around in their minds, but their ideas seldom traveled from their head to the paper.

They could easily tell me about the concepts they had for their 'master-pieces,' but few of them had even the first ten pages written down. Their time was spread thin between their classes, family, friends, jobs, and life in general. Does this sound familiar? Without the ability to schedule their time and connect a series of productive days, they were incapable of completing a goal, even one they were supposedly passionate about.

They knew their destination, but never found a vehicle to take them there. No matter what state you live in, even the best car will not get you to Hawaii! The choice of a vehicle is always vital to your success. The right vehicle will allow you to complete your journey over the next 90 days. If your destination is important to you, and I am confident that it is of great importance, then choosing the right vehicle, to help you optimize your time, will guarantee your arrival.

You have already learned the importance of scheduling your day and you know the power of a 90-day period of time. But, for you to stay on track and accomplish your goals, you must optimize your next 90 days. Your G.P.S. (Goal Planning Strategy) is your vehicle to do just that.

Taking the time and effort to transform your thoughts into a written plan is no small task. By physically seeing your goals on paper, you create an edge. That edge becomes an advantage as you develop a plan to accomplish them. But, it will be your ability to implement a strategy, to stay the course when your boat is rocked, that will give you the power you need to complete your *90 Day Run.*

Throughout this book, you have been completing each of the five steps necessary to accomplish your goals. Now, it's time to transfer this information into one comprehensive program to structure your actions and accomplish your goals during your *90 Day Run.*

G.P.S.– GOAL PLANNING STRATEGY

- **GOAL**: Accomplish goals which are life-changing and remarkable in magnitude and degree.
- **PLANNING**: Identify the path to follow in order to achieve greatness.
- **STRATEGY**: Implement your plan, especially when obstacles are in your way.

Your G.P.S. has been designed to be much more than just a vehicle to help you get to your destination. It is a business plan, a blueprint, a road map, and a personal motivator all wrapped up into one dynamic tool, developed to allow you to see your big picture.

You can accomplish much in a well-defined block of time, if you follow the right program! Boot camp utilized a 90-day time period for our training, but it was the optimization of each day that allowed us to accomplish great things. You cannot arrive at your destination instantly, but you can change your direction immediately!

Your written goals are only the beginning. Your G.P.S. will help you prioritize what you do each day. It is an effective forum for entering, tracking, measuring, and course-correcting your actions during your

90 Day Run. It will provide you with the direction and clarification necessary to achieve a greater life.

Your completed G.P.S. will be a source of motivation and inspiration as you take each step toward your goals. It is your contract and commitment to yourself; a commitment to achieve a greater life. Each day, as you implement and review your personal G.P.S., you will see in full detail:

- Your well-defined short-term and long-term goals
- Your high expectations
- Actions you must take
- Timelines for completion
- A daily planner to keep you on track
- Progress reports to measure your success

Let the abundant power of your Goal Planning Strategy fuel your *90 Day Run* and lead you to a greater life. Within 90 days, you will transform many areas of your life. Each *90 Day Run* allows you to review your performance, enhance your strengths, and overcome your weaknesses. Your G.P.S. will provide you with the structure you need to get the results you desire.

A GREAT IDEA

I had been thinking about my greater purpose for months. I knew that I wanted to help people accomplish life-changing goals – no matter what circumstances they faced. But I had no idea how I would start doing it. On Saturdays, I would venture to my local coffee shop to get my juices flowing. But, how would I turn my greater purpose into a reality?

For a few weeks, I searched my heart for the right direction. But, each day I went back home empty handed. Gina would reassuringly tell me, "I know you'll come up with something." The following Saturday, I sat there for about an hour. My pen had remained unmoved and my pad of paper looked brand new. Not a single inspiring thought entered my head on 'how' to help people.

I kept thinking to myself, "I need to think of something great." Well, that was a start, so I wrote "need to think of something great" on my all-too-clean notepad. I looked back at the words a few minutes later. Two words stood out: *'think'* and *'great'*. That was it, I needed to teach people how to *think great*. I finally had the idea. I would write a book called Think GREAT!

I rushed home to share my idea with Gina. I could tell, by the look on her face, that a book about thinking great was the way to go. But, I had never written a book before. Gina asked the logical question, "How are you going to write a book?" I did not have the answer to that, so I researched book writing online and discovered that there was a general consensus that it takes about an hour to write one page.

I had a fairly hectic schedule, so I set up a *90 Day Run* to accomplish that goal. I would use my G.P.S. to help me complete a page per day of my book. I scheduled each day and optimized my time for 90 days, but I ended up with more than 90 pages. I had written 160. By using the power of my G.P.S., I nearly doubled my short-term goal. I connected another *90 Day Run* and set out to accomplish my long-term goal of completing my book.

By using my G.P.S. again, I completed the first draft of my book during my next 90 days. It was 268 pages and ready to be published! My G.P.S. did much more than help take the steps toward my goal, it allowed me to take the steps toward my greater purpose. If the 'writers' I met in college had planned their days properly and dedicated the adequate time to write one page per day, they could have completed their books, novels, plays, and scripts.

How many days and weeks have gone by without you accomplishing your life-changing goals? Learning how to optimize your time is critical to achieving a greater life. As you accomplish specific goals in one area of your life, the benefits will have a domino effect and also help you to accomplish goals in other areas. By scheduling your days and maximizing your time, you are capable of accomplishing your short-term goals in 90 days!

YOUR G.P.S. PROVIDES BALANCE

Imagine that you have the goal of walking in a straight line. Accomplishing that goal sounds simple, right? What if your environment changes? Now, imagine taking those same steps on a small boat, in the middle of the ocean. The steps are the same, but they are not as easy to take.

Now, imagine trying to take those same steps as the waves rise and rock your boat back and forth. The steps have still not changed, but their level of difficulty has increased. Most people stop taking the simple steps toward their goals as soon as their lives get a little off balance.

Your *Goal Planning Strategy* provides a solid foundation to take every step necessary, regardless of what difficulties rock your boat. I use my G.P.S. to support each step I take, for every goal I pursue. Your G.P.S. provides the proper balance between your challenges and your big picture. By paying close attention to your time, your motivation, and your impact on others, you will determine the success of your goals.

THE BENEFIT OF YOUR G.P.S.

Documenting your results and course-correcting are crucial to elevating your results. The level of greatness you reach is directly related to the level of detail you put into your G.P.S. In sports, athletes and their coaches keep detailed records of every action they take, on and off the court. Coaches and players consistently review the 'tape' of the last game or performance.

With much at stake, they analyze every movement an athlete makes. Making the necessary course-corrections allows them to run faster, throw the ball more accurately, or make that game-winning shot. It can mean the difference between winning and losing. It can mean the difference between the gold medal and the silver medal. It can mean an advantage of one hundredth of a second.

At the Beijing Olympics in 2008, it came down to just that. Michael Phelps won his seventh gold medal by the smallest unit of measurement in swimming; one hundredth of a second! In fact, from August 10 to August 17, 2008, Michael won a total of eight gold medals, broke seven world records, and one Olympic record. By the end of the games, the 23-year-old swimmer had sixteen Olympic medals to his name, fourteen of them gold! No one else in the history of the Olympics has won as many medals.

Michael had his challenges too. He was diagnosed with Attention-Deficit Hyperactivity Disorder (ADHD) at an early age and was encouraged to take up swimming as a way to provide an outlet for his energy. At the age of eleven, he caught the attention of Bob Bowman, a former college swimmer who also had a degree in child psychology. Coach Bowman recognized Michael's skills, but left nothing to chance. He encouraged Michael to swim at least 50 miles each week.

He noted that this type of training would increase the size of his heart and lungs, in ways that would be impossible as he got older. To this day, one of Michael's greatest strengths is his endurance. Under the watchful eye of Coach Bowman, Michael continues to train daily for up to five hours in the water, even on his birthday and Christmas! The intense training requires a high calorie diet. He regularly consumes up to 12,000 calories per day, while the average man consumes 2,500.

Michael also trained with weights, which was also closely monitored. His first weight trainer put him on a routine that started to increase his muscle mass, which is counter-productive for a swimmer. He was quickly replaced with a trainer who developed a more swimmer-friendly routine, focusing on muscle endurance and flexibility. Michael's training also included the use of a stationary bike for cardiovascular exercise, because running could damage his knees.

He competes in a variety of swimming events, each with different strokes and lengths. Each event requires careful planning and a detailed strategy to win! Both Michael and Coach Bowman meticulously focus on his swimming techniques and analyze everything to find areas to correct and improve upon. As they prepare for the next Olympics, Michael and his coach will focus on analyzing his activities on a daily basis, to add to his already impressive collection of gold medals.

SUCCESSFULLY COMPLETING YOUR G.P.S.

I have seen people accomplish their goals by using forms, charts, calendars, journals, and online management tools to plan out their time and strategize their actions. I have saved you the time of creating them on your own and designed effective templates to help you develop your G.P.S. for your personal *90 Day Run*.

Setting up your Goal Planning Strategy is such an exciting process! Investing time in the development of this tool will ensure that all of the valuable information necessary for a successful *90 Day Run* has been entered. Your G.P.S. will provide you with eight unique components that, when combined, will elevate your ability to accomplish any goal you desire.

Individual components of your G.P.S.:

1. **Personal Contract**
2. **Overview of your *90 Day Run***
3. **Short-Term Goal List**
4. **G.R.E.A.T. Goal List**
5. **Goal Status Sheet**
6. **Daily Action Planner**
7. **Daily Journal**
8. **GREAT Achievements**

During your run, I will be your Goal Coach, helping you every step of the way. I will help you stay on track and achieve greatness on many levels. Chapter 13 will provide you with each of the templates for a successful run. It will also feature examples of a completed G.P.S. as an added benefit.

As you complete each of the eight components of your G.P.S., be as detailed as possible. A clearly defined plan will help you orchestrate all your actions and create momentum, even before your *90 Day Run* starts! A detailed G.P.S. will start to work on your mind, which will cause your mind to start working on your goals.

If you are like me, you are ready to complete your G.P.S. and start your *90 Day Run*. You now understand The 5 Steps to Accomplishing Goals and the importance of Time Mastery. But there is one final piece to this puzzle. I did not go through boot camp alone. Your *90 Day Run* will be most effective if you harness the power of people, starting with yourself!

GREAT Exercises

Maximize Your Time

Your *90 Day Run* is about making the most out of your time. For one day, log in everything you do. At the end of the day, review your data and determine if there are activities you should eliminate or add to help you achieve greatness.

* Keep track of everything, even things you know you will need to change (donuts and coffee for breakfast).

EXAMPLE:

6:30 am   Woke Up - got ready for work
7:00 am   Grabbed a donut & coffee
8:00 am   Dropped the kids off at school
8:15 am   Commuted to work
9:00 am   Started work

Slow Down to Speed Up

Identify areas of your life that currently take up too much of your time to complete. Then list what you can do to make these areas more efficient, so you can dedicate that extra time to accomplishing your goals.

Part III

You Never Run Alone

Part III

You Never Run Alone

Everyone Can Use a Little Support!

There have been times when I tried to pursue my life- changing goals alone, but I have never accomplished one by myself. Unless you live on a desert island, you are going to encounter people on a daily basis. Each day, they have the ability to influence your life, whether you are striving for a greater one or not. Their involvement can have a major impact on your ability to accomplish your goals. The final element of *The GOAL Formula* is People.

In boot camp, our drill instructors positioned each recruit in a squad. Each squad consisted of twelve recruits, with a squad leader at the front. All four squads comprised our platoon, with a guide to lead the way. Our platoon was connected with two other platoons, which formed a series. Our series was part of another series, which formed our company. Each week, the Marine Corps graduates one company from boot camp. We trained together and graduated together. The goal of becoming a Marine was a team effort.

When other people help you to accomplish life-changing goals, the positive results are never limited to just you. The process affects them as well. But here is the best part; the benefits do not start after you accomplish the goals, they start immediately as you begin to pursue them. Accomplishing even a minor goal can achieve major results for everyone involved.

Team work is crucial for accomplishing goals, but people are not the only ones who understand this advantage. Have you ever noticed that geese fly in a 'V' formation? Their journey is of great importance. In fact, their lives depend on it. Geese migrate to find better temperatures, more food, and to reproduce. To arrive at their destination, they may fly over one thousand miles. When goals are this important, you do everything you can to ensure success.

The V-Formation and your *90 Day Run* have many similarities:

V-Formation	90 Day Run
The flock accomplishes at least 71% greater flying range than any bird flying alone!	By working with others, you will increase your odds of making it to your destination.
When the lead goose gets tired, another goose takes over.	It helps to have someone who will make sure you do not lose momentum.
Geese in the back, honk to encourage those in the front.	Sometimes we can all use some encouragement to keep us motivated!
If one of the geese is injured or becomes sick and falls out of formation, two geese will stay behind until that goose can rejoin the formation, or it dies!	If your goals are important to others, in addition to yourself, you can achieve a greater life, even if you cannot always make it by yourself.

I always found it interesting that geese figured out the power of working with others, but people often struggle with it. The right people can help you get the results you are looking for. So, when you are on the quest for a greater life, be sure to understand that You Never Run Alone.

Too often, people abandon their goals because they feel like they are on the journey alone. When it comes to achieving great things, everyone needs a little help. Even the *Lone Ranger* had *Tonto*, and he needed his assistance in every episode!

To guarantee that You Never Run Alone, develop your *Goal Team* by focusing on three key points.

1. **Your Belief Level**
2. **Your Personal Network**
3. **Your GREAT Partner**

By properly incorporating your Belief Level, Personal Network, and GREAT Partner, you will take your life to a new level. We seldom experience substantial rewards and satisfaction by accomplishing our goals alone. When we achieve greatness in our lives, it will inevitably affect the lives of others in an amazingly positive way.

One of the most powerful resources available for accomplishing goals is people, but it is often the most underused. Achieving a greater life for yourself is rarely accomplished by yourself. While you are responsible for taking the steps to accomplishing goals, your *90 Day Run* will be more successful if you understand how to harness the power of people.

To ensure that You Never Run Alone, focus on gaining the support of the people in your life, starting with yourself. You are the key to your success. Your ability to enlist the help of others will be determined by your commitment to your own *90 Day Run* and your belief level.

Chapter 10

Your Belief Level

You Are the Secret to Your Success!

What is the difference between being in a slump and being in a grave? Being in a slump is depressing, but you can get out by yourself. In fact, it is the only way! People can help you, even encourage you, but overcoming whatever circumstance you face is ultimately your choice. When it comes to moving ahead in life, many people feel they are in a slump, day in and day out. The same job, the same commute, the same everything – everyday!

Adding the accomplishment of life-changing goals can seem overwhelming to many people. By developing a strong belief level, you can climb out of any slump you are in. Your belief level not only allows you to see your destination in full detail, before taking any steps, but it creates a vivid image of you having already arrived.

Your mind is the greatest tool you possess for accomplishing your goals. But, too many people try to build a greater life without using the mind's true potential. The only limitations you have are the ones you believe. Success and failure are both the result of your belief level. So, what is belief level? It is a combination of your passion and your perception.

Passion + Perception = Belief Level

Passion – desiring to achieve it.

+

Perception – envisioning that you will achieve it.

=

Belief Level – believing that you have already achieved it!

There is no doubt that you are passionate about your goals, and I am confident that you have a focused perception about your ability to accomplishing them. By focusing on your passion and enhancing your perception, you will strengthen your belief level.

My circumstances often clouded my mind and made it more difficult to accomplish my goals. It was easy for my mind to drift from our dreams to our nightmares. But there was a lot riding on my ability to accomplish our goals. So, I developed other options for my mind to concentrate on; options that helped me to create a belief level so strong, that nothing would keep me from my goals. You can choose to use these options too.

POINT A TO POINT B

At the beginning of Gina's chemotherapy treatments, we learned a great deal about the horrific effects that the poison would have on her body. But we also discovered a statistic that caused us to put our passion at the forefront of our lives. We found out that many marriages fall apart when a spouse battles cancer. Even though they may beat the disease, the marriage can die shortly after. Couples often have to endure more hardships, while experiencing less intimacy, or sometimes, no intimacy.

Certain types of cancer, such as cervical and testicular cancer, can heighten the risk of divorce. Women with cervical cancer are 70% more likely to get divorced and men with testicular cancer are 34% more likely. Just knowing these facts better prepared us to handle our situation.

If you have lived through a battle with a life-threatening disease, you know how challenging it can be: mentally, physically, and emotionally. We certainly felt the increased hardships and experienced the decreased intimacy. But we were passionate about keeping the spark in our relationship alive. Our marriage was the most stable aspect we had. We could not afford for it to fall apart.

In addition to our other goals, we set the goal of keeping our marriage strong. To make sure that we accomplished this goal we used a simple concept that was based on our passion. I call it "Point A to Point B." We knew the times ahead would be difficult and challenging. We also knew that there would be many unknown obstacles coming our way.

Just days after her diagnosis, Gina and I made a simple commitment to each other. We chose to make the most of our journey, all the way from Point A to Point B, no matter where our Point B took us. We made a pact to stay positive! Our passion to keep our marriage intact became an underlying source of power for us.

Just because you cannot see your Point B, does not mean you should stand still on your Point A. In Gina's case, going from Point A to Point B, with the best possible attitude, was critical for her survival.

During her treatments we met many other people who were battling cancer. Unfortunately, not all of them made it and we lost some good friends along the way. This caused us to focus on our Point A to Point B commitment even more! No matter how tough it got, we kept a positive attitude and refused to give up.

The difference between wanting something and needing something will be a determining factor in attaining your goals. Passion convinces you that your goals are worth fighting for. But, a burning passion will guarantee that you stay the course and will also attract others to you. The stronger your passion, the more people will be attracted to help support your efforts.

PASSION BUILDS STRENGTH

Without a genuine passion for something, you will resort to the same kind of excuses and denial that have caused you to avoid a greater life in the past. Passion causes you to change your habits and will carry you through the tough times. If passion burns strong enough, any goal is achievable. Passion also allows you to have fun, even during difficult times.

Gina's battle with cancer did not end as she went into remission. The first year was the actual fight to survive. During this time, she received chemotherapy, radiation treatments and a stem cell transplant. It was chaotic, but it was controlled chaos. I felt that my tour of duty in the

Marine Corps helped prepare me to handle this time period in our lives. But for us, the most challenging part was the recovery phase.

Just after she started to recover, Gina was readmitted to the City of Hope because the doctors thought her brain was bleeding. Luckily, it was not her brain. Odd as it sounds, we were relieved to find out her lungs were bleeding. Imagine receiving that kind of news and being relieved about it! She remained at the City of Hope for another two weeks. We rarely went anywhere for the next two years because Gina would get exhausted very easily. Even simple actions such as going to the store, exhausted most of her energy.

It took over two years for Gina to regain her strength. She was on different types of medications, each with serious side-effects, which the next prescription was supposed to alleviate. It seemed like a never-ending chain reaction and our bathroom counter was starting to look like a pharmacy.

The drugs often caused Gina to have horrible mood swings. During the difficult recovery times, she did not sound like the girl I had married. But who was I to say anything to her? After all, she had battled cancer, and won. I knew it was not Gina talking to me like that, it was her medication.

These were the hardest times on our marriage. These were the times that were the most challenging for both of us. So, we kept our Point A to Point B commitment at the forefront of our discussions. Without our burning passion for each other, I am not sure where our marriage would have ended up.

By attaching the Point A to Point B technique to our lives, we kept our marriage together and stayed on track to accomplishing our other goals as well.

PERCEPTION

The problem that most people encounter is that they cannot see the path to a greater life. That does not mean that it is not there, just that they do not see it. So, they fail to take any steps. Perception is how you *see* your circumstances.

Your perception allows you to visualize your 'completed' goals, before you complete them. Visualizing your goals always precedes realizing your goals. It will not only allow you to see clearly during the dark times, but it will provide direction for your future, by showing you what to focus on.

Your perception can be positive or negative; strong or weak. If you intend to accomplish your goals, you must harness the power of a positive perception. People tend to have a great perception during good times. It is during the bad times that their perception often shifts. Gina and I made the decision to change our perception about 'bad' times.

We started to look at 'BAD' times as opportunities to grow and to start over with a clean slate. Here is our definition of 'BAD.'

B.A.D. = Begin Again Differently

Do not just turn your lemons into lemonade. Use *The GOAL Formula* and turn them into a lemon meringue pie!

MY BELIEF LEVEL

A strong belief level will let you know, without question, that you will succeed in whatever you put your mind to. I had the deep passion to become a Marine and my perception allowed me to see the completion of my goal. But it was my belief level that helped me to get back on my horse, after my first night in boot camp knocked me off.

During the three hours since our arrival, we had turned in our civilian clothes, been issued our camouflage uniforms, stenciled our names onto everything, and had our heads shaved. Oh, did I mention there was also a lot of yelling? We had volumes of colorful language thrown at us from two of the loudest men I had ever encountered.

As mad as these two 'processing' drill instructors seemed, they were kind enough to let us know that we would only be with them for about one week while we were completing our paperwork, getting our gear issued, and receiving our vaccination shots.

After that week, we would be handed off to our 'training' drill instructors – a much louder, more intense group of Marines who would see to it that all of the 'non-hackers' were weeded out, and only the 'hard-chargers' would graduate. Would I be one of these hard-chargers? I was nervous, concerned, and afraid. Where had my passion and perception gone to?

Late that first night I was lying motionless on the top rack of my bunk, but I was unable to sleep. I kept thinking, "What have I done?" Three weeks earlier, I had turned eighteen and was hanging out with my friends back home, with no worries. But right now, I was in Marine Corps boot camp!

When we first arrived, we were convincingly told, "Not everyone of you will make it." What if I was one of the recruits who would not make it? What would my drill instructors do to me if I failed? What would my father think of me? What would my younger brother think? How would I feel about myself? To say that I was worried would be an understatement.

Fear filled my mind in a way I have never experienced. I was afraid of the unknown. I was afraid of what tomorrow would bring. I was afraid of not graduating. What if I never made it out of boot camp? I had only been there for a few hours and I already knew I wanted to leave. The first three hours seemed difficult enough, but the uncertainties of the next three months put a pit in my stomach.

My circumstances felt so overwhelming that I had stopped focusing on my goal. Graduating from recruit training seemed like an insurmountable objective. I tried to sleep, knowing that we would be starting our day in just a few short hours. I was exhausted, but my eyes would not stay shut.

It was eerily silent in the barracks. The moonlight shining in the windows was just enough to allow me to see the others sleeping in their bunks. I sat up and a simple thought entered my head. As I looked at my fellow recruits, I thought, "most of them will graduate, so why not me?" I did the math: each week, 300 new recruits graduate from Marine Corps boot camp in San Diego, California. That is about 15,000 per year!

More recruits graduate from the Marines Corps' other boot camp in Parris Island, South Carolina. I realized that from the time of my birth until I was eighteen years old, over half a million recruits, just like me, earned the title of U.S. Marine. I dwelled further on that thought and felt an immediate relief from the fear and worry. Understanding that others have already accomplished the same goal I was pursuing, strengthened my belief level. I felt my passion swell and my perception change.

As boot camp progressed, new challenges came my way, but I continued to have a strong belief level. Three months later, I graduated with a platoon of forty-eight. Our drill instructors were right; not everyone made it! Because of my belief level, I did.

IF THEY CAN DO IT, SO CAN I

When it comes to accomplishing goals, my belief level is, "If they can do it, so can I." It has empowered me and given me the confidence to achieve greatness in any area of my life! You can use this same principle to enhance your belief level, which will keep your passion alive and your perception sharp.

Every time I set a goal, I take a close look at it and try to imagine how many other people have already accomplished it. Take a look at some of the goals you have listed so far. How many of them have been successfully accomplished by someone else?

If one of your goals is to minimize debt, you can easily find examples of people who have reduced their debt, or perhaps eliminated it. If you want to lose weight, there are thousands of people who have shed pounds, perhaps the exact amount you need to. Even if your goal is to go to the moon, others have already done it.

Are they any better than you? No, of course not. Is their belief level stronger? Maybe, but not for long. If they can do it, so can you. A strong belief level keeps you in control of your thoughts. When you control your thoughts, you control your life!

CHOOSING TO BELIEVE

If you could analyze the belief levels of those who have achieved greatness in their lives, you would find that they have one thing in common. Success was not so much what they did; it was what they believed they could do. What you choose to think about will greatly affect your belief level. When you choose to have a strong belief level, you choose to have a great life.

No one is destined to either good luck or bad luck. But that does not stop some people from believing that the only luck they have is bad. You do not have to believe anything that does not serve your greater purpose! Choosing the belief level you have is what defines your luck! End of story. Think differently about luck and your luck will change.

Gina and I rarely had the opportunity to define our relationship by the good times. When I made the decision to write this book, my goal was to provide a comprehensive guide to accomplishing goals – no matter what circumstance you face. One month after writing the first page, Gina was diagnosed again. This time with breast cancer.

Ironically, the radiation treatments she received ten years ago to fight cancer, ended up giving her breast cancer. Through this entire month, Gina had the weight of her new cancer on her mind, but it did not stop her from helping me to write this book in between her medical appointments.

These are challenging times, but our passion and our perception have helped us to have a strong belief level. We choose to believe that there was a reason for her to have cancer again. We are confident that it is part of our greater purpose. Did we have a hard time with the news? Yes. Was she afraid? Without a doubt. Did we regroup and focus on our belief level? Absolutely! Our belief level dictated how we handled her situation.

Because you cannot receive radiation in the same area twice, her only option was a mastectomy. Just two hours after I took her to the hospital her surgeon performed the operation. My wife had one of her breasts removed, but not her fighting spirit. She shares my passion for helping people and is determined to take more steps toward our goals.

What do you have on your plate today? Are you going to give it the power to keep you from moving forward? Everyone can be energetic and excited when they have no financial worries, health concerns, or personal issues to overcome. Our marriage has never been defined by eating at a fancy restaurant during the good times. Our marriage was defined when Gina and I ate dinner in her hospital room on Valentine's Day, February 14, 2000.

NEVER LEAVE ROOM FOR DOUBT

There is an old adage that says, "Actions speak louder than words." But "Belief level speaks louder than both," is more accurate. Your thoughts are more powerful than your actions, because it is your thoughts that dictate your actions. Not the other way around.

Your belief level will shape your life from this moment forward, by providing you with an unmatched level of confidence, a positive attitude, and a crystal-clear vision. Imagine what you could accomplish if you always had these three areas functioning at high levels simultaneously! I cannot stress the importance of your belief level enough. If it is strong, you can accomplish your goals – no matter what circumstances you face!

Belief levels feed off of the dominant thoughts that occupy your mind. If you believe you will not achieve a greater life, you are absolutely correct. Believing you can achieve greatness is a critical step toward being prepared for it. Those with strong belief levels are not afraid to move forward because they view moments of failure, or challenge, as opportunities for growth and improvement.

Your belief level focuses on what your mind envisions. You will either see yourself accomplishing your goal or see yourself missing it. Your vision will transform your thoughts into reality. Visualizing your goals will take your *90 Day Run* to a new level. In fact, it will take your life to a new level.

Before becoming an international movie star, actor/comedian Jim Carrey worked with his family in security and janitorial jobs at a factory to make a living. For a short period, they even lived in their van!

During these difficult times, he visualized his goal with great detail. His belief level was so strong that he wrote a check to himself for $20 million and kept it in his wallet for years, determined to eventually earn that amount. In 1996, Jim Carrey was paid $20 million to star in *The Cable Guy*, becoming the first actor to receive a salary of that level for a single movie!

Never leave room for doubt. If you do, it will creep in and eventually dominate all of your thoughts. To keep your belief level strong, repeat powerful statements to yourself as often as you can. Try saying, "I will get my promotion at work" twice per day, or "I will lose 25 pounds." Only you can control the thoughts that flow through your mind. As soon as you accept that the only person responsible for who and where you are is you, the sooner you can step forward.

NEVER STOP BELIEVING

Bringing a new life into the world has, by far, been the greatest experience in my life. Being a parent has always been natural to me. I love being a dad to my two sons and looked forward to sharing that experience with Gina. After we were married, we had planned on having children together within a few years. It was Gina's dream to have a little girl of her own.

When the doctors told us that she would be unable to have children due to the effects of her treatments, it was devastating. We were given enough depressing news during her fight with cancer, but this was one of the worst by far. And it deeply crushed her spirit.

The doctors believed that Gina would never be able to have children. They explained to us the effects that the chemotherapy and stem cell transplant would have on her body, and even pointed out that the radiation treatments had partially 'melted' some of her internal organs. They made a pretty convincing case, not leaving us any hope.

Looking at Gina, you would think that they were right. She weighed just over a hundred pounds; she was bald and delicately frail. It would have been easy for us to believe them, but I knew the power of a strong belief level. We had a shared goal: having a baby girl. We never gave up hope.

At one point, we were told that Gina would never speak again because the cancer had paralyzed her vocal cords. Three months later, she had her full voice back. The doctors were wrong about that, perhaps they were wrong about her not being able to have children.

We kept talking about having a child of our own and picturing a little one running through our home. We would talk about different names and often found ourselves in baby departments looking at everything from little pink dresses to furniture for the nursery.

Seven years after being diagnosed, Gina was well-past the critical five-year mark in her remission. She continued to get a clean bill of health and had been cancer-free long enough that her check-ups were decreased to only once per year. Life moved on. We still believed that one day, Gina would be a mom, but we discussed it less and less as each year passed by.

A few weeks before each annual check-up, we would both tend to get a little nervous, anxious to hear that Gina was still cancer-free. She always called me as soon as her results were in. I remember one call in particular. It was Tuesday, January 3rd, 2006, and I was in my office when my phone rang. Her doctor had run two different tests. I was relieved to find out that the first test results came back negative for cancer. Then she said that her additional test results came back positive... for pregnancy!

I laughed a little and waited for her to laugh back, but Gina remained quiet. Her silence said so much! I was speechless. We had continued to believe that one day she would be pregnant, and that one day was here! Gina was pregnant! We truly appreciated every moment of her pregnancy. It was such an unbelievable sound to hear the tiny little heartbeat during the ultrasound sessions. I watched in sheer amazement, as Gina's once frail body became filled with another life.

She had a glow that I had never seen before. We had been together for ten years, and I was looking at a new woman! Her smile could not have been bigger, when the ultrasound technician told us we were going to have a baby girl! It was truly a dream come true. It happened, even though we had been told that it was virtually impossible. Gina's body took the actions necessary to get in alignment with her unwavering Belief Level.

I have never experienced anything greater than seeing my little angel handed to her mommy after delivery. It was amazing to witness this miracle right before my eyes. What if Gina had stopped believing?

A strong belief level forces you to make the changes in your life necessary to align yourself with your goals. Too many people waste valuable time searching for the 'secret' of success? The secret is you! Never stop believing in you. Develop a strong belief level now.

Chapter 11

Your Personal Network

Harness the Power of People!

No one goes through boot camp alone. It was always a group (platoon) effort. I was fortunate to be surrounded by so many other people who supported my actions. My personal network included my fellow recruits, who were focused on the same goal that I was. My drill instructors were part of that network and provided additional resources and assistance. In fact, everyone on the base was a valuable member of my Personal Network. They all helped me to accomplish my goal of becoming a Marine.

Having other people support your actions puts a sense of urgency on the accomplishment of your goals. A personal network focused on your success will help you to develop good habits and break bad habits at a faster pace. Trust me; it is much easier to break a bad habit if you know that your entire platoon will receive a penalty, not just you. The last thing I wanted to do was to let my platoon down.

More than likely, your life does not have the intense personal network that we had in boot camp. Far too many people fail to set up a successful personal network to assist with their *90 Day Run*. Some people give up on their goals because they attempt to pursue them alone, while others give up because of the negative impact that another person has had.

TYPES OF PEOPLE

People play an important role in your life, especially during the next 90 days. I have pursued goals in different areas of my life and have met many different people along the way. Each person was unique and had an impact in my life, in one way or another. Regardless of how different everyone was, when considering their support of my goals, I found that they fell into four categories. Since I have a passion for the movies, we will relate their roles to the flicks!

Action Heroes

Action heroes push you into action and encourage you to go after your goals. They believe in you, sometimes more than you may believe in yourself. They take your goals as seriously as you do. They provide you with motivation when you need it the most, and they often encourage you to take the risks necessary to achieve a greater life. They may not always follow the script, but they complete the scene!

Directors

Directors understand the essence of your goals. They may have even helped you develop them. They provide you with valuable guidance and direction. They may even help enlist other people to enhance the strength of your personal network.

Audience Members

The audience knows that you are striving for the Oscar, but usually are there just to watch the show. They are 'for' you, but they may not be able to do a lot 'for' you. Although they may do little more than just watch the show, they will cheer for you when you accomplish a goal. Their support can be meaningful from time to time.

Critics

As they say, "Those who can, do; those who can't, criticize." The name says it all. Critics usually do not pursue their own goals and are often uncomfortable that you are pursuing yours. Typically, 'Critics' do not give positive reviews. You can anticipate their thumbs pointing down and they may shoot down every one of your performances.

It should be your objective to invest as much time as possible with the Action Heroes and the Directors in your life. Work with the audience members when it benefits you. Stay away from the Critics. There is too much at stake to waste time with the wrong people.

ANNOUNCE YOUR GOALS

One of the first benefits you will experience by identifying your Personal Network is that it will allow you to increase your pace to accomplishing your goals, by shining the 'spotlight' on your *90 Day Run*. Make a list of all of the people you can announce your goals to. Of course, you may not be able to let everyone know every goal – some things may be too personal.

You can list your parents, brothers and sisters, children, aunts and uncles, friends, and co-workers. The more people who know of your goals, the more likely you are to accomplish them. To turn up the heat even more, let everyone on the list know the timelines of each of your goals. You will find that they will ask you about them to make sure you are on track. If you are like me, you will want to have the right answer when they call.

When I found out that I would be graduating from boot camp on November 13, 1987, I was so excited that I wrote to my parents and my friends. They were all excited too. They told me that they were all coming to San Diego for my graduation ceremony. That put some pressure on me. I still had to make it out of Phase 1 and complete Phases 2 and 3! But, it gave me an extra incentive to graduate. I was not as worried about failing as I was about letting down my family and friends.

Announce your goals and timelines to your Personal Network.

A GREAT GOAL REQUIRES A GREAT TEAM

Some people have had the goal of climbing Mount Everest, the highest mountain on earth. It reaches 29,029 feet above sea level. At that elevation there is only one-third of the oxygen available as there is at sea-level. The temperature gets low enough that any exposed skin will get frostbite. Exhaustion quickly sets in for many under these extreme conditions.

Nevertheless, many have tried to climb Mount Everest, but few accomplished it. In fact, some never made it off of the mountain. It is common that climbers who die during the ascent are left on the trail. In fact, there are more than 150 bodies still up there, many visible from the routes used to ascend the mountain.

I have no desire to climb Mount Everest. It is not one of my goals. But if it were, I would make sure that I was not doing it alone. I would choose to have someone with me who had successfully done it before! Remember, "If someone else can do it, so can you!" For me, climbing Mount Everest would be an extreme way to test this statement, but if I did, I would very carefully pick my personal network.

In 1953, a British expedition attempted the ascent and they chose their personal network with great care. Edmund Hillary, the leader of the expedition, had the goal to be the first to make it to the top, but he did not attempt it alone. He had a Director in his corner, John Hunt, who led the expedition teams. He had Audience Members carrying equipment and setting up camp, and he had his fair share of Critics, who said it could never be done.

But, most importantly, Edmund Hillary had an Action Hero who was critical to his success. This man was a Sherpa named Tenzing Norgay. Sherpas live in the mountainous region of Nepal. They are regarded as elite mountaineers and have the physical endurance to handle the extreme altitude and conditions of Mount Everest.

Sherpas are almost synonymous with climbing Mount Everest. Expeditions which do not employ Sherpas as their guides do not achieve greatness. Properly enlisting the help of his personal network allowed Edmund Hillary to be the first person to reach the summit. He arrived at 11:30 am on May 29, 1953; two days after the first team on his expedition had turned back due to exhaustion.

TAKE YOUR OWN STEPS

One of the biggest mistakes people make when trying to achieve a greater life is hoping that others will do it for them. Even though Tenzing Norgay led the way to the top of Mount Everest with his expertise, he did not carry Edmund Hillary. Edmund took each step on his own.

When my daughter was two years old, she preferred that I carried her up the stairs, even though she was capable of walking on her own. I would encourage her to climb up herself and I was right there to support her, every step of the way. She 'wanted' to get to the top of the stairs quickly, but she 'needed' Daddy to carry her. She was a cute toddler and it was difficult for me to tell her 'No.' So, she often got her way and I ended up carrying her.

Getting carried is cute when you are two, but not when you are pursuing greatness as an adult. On your journey to a greater life, find people who have achieved goals similar to yours and incorporate them into your personal network. I am always surprised when I see whom people choose to help them accomplish their 'life-changing' goals. I have seen broke people giving financial advice, and people who are out of shape training others in the gym. If you want to be Mr. Olympia, do not ask Pee Wee Herman for body-building tips.

HELPING OTHERS HELPS YOU

It is healthy to forget about focusing on yourself from time to time and to apply your efforts to helping others, particularly your Personal Network. The act of helping others benefits you and improves your well-being, making it easier to accomplish your goals. Doing great things for others not only positively impacts you mentally, but positively impacts you physically as well.

It is similar to the feeling that runners commonly experience after running certain distances. Engaging in moderately intense exercise for at least twenty minutes releases endorphins by the pituitary gland in your brain. This creates a physical phenomenon often referred to as a 'Runner's High.'

This natural 'high' can create a feeling of euphoria, reducing emotional reactions to stress, and keeping the individual in a great mood. This is a welcome 'high' with no negative side effects. I absolutely do not like to run, but the Marine Corps does. As a Marine, I went on plenty of runs during my tour of duty, and I experienced the 'Runner's High' many times, usually around mile two.

Helping your Personal Network to achieve greatness can have a similar effect on you. Our brain is a unique tool – *remarkable in magnitude and degree!* You can get your brain to work for you by putting the needs of others before your own needs. When you do, you will trigger powerful chemical reactions in your brain, which will help with your energy level and motivation.

One of the reasons people enjoy receiving rewards is that our brains produce a chemical called dopamine upon receiving something positive. In fact, dopamine neurons even become active in anticipation of receiving it. Hence, we are geared to repeat behaviors which cause us to receive positive rewards.

Studies show that the same physiological 'euphoric' state that occurs when we receive a reward also happens when we give a reward. This chemical reaction creates another phenomenon often referred to as a 'Helper's High.'

Do not merely expect help from your Personal Network, provide it to them as well. Allow the benefit of supporting others to help support your *90 Day Run*.

AN EDUCATION IN HELPING OTHERS

Because it is now understood that the process of giving helps to increase personal performance, the State Education Agency K-12 Service-Learning Network (SEANet) has started to use it for students. SEANet is a national network committed to advancing school-based service-learning initiatives in K-12 schools across the country. Schools receive state formula grants from Learn and Serve America, the primary federal funding source for service-learning.

SEANet focuses on this technique because the positive effect of helping others increases the personal performance of the students involved. Many high schools require their students to participate in service-learning. Teachers have observed that the students who volunteer raise their grades and get higher SAT scores. Interestingly enough, the results are positive even when the charity work is not voluntary. Students who were 'forced' to help others also had an increase in their performance and test results.

Harvard University even conducted a study of this phenomenon and called it the 'Mother Teresa Effect.' In their study, researchers showed 132 Harvard students a film about Mother Teresa's charity work. The students had their levels of Immunoglobulin A measured before and after watching the film.

Immunoglobulin A is an anti-body which plays a critical role as the body's first defense against the common cold virus. The results showed dramatically increased levels of the anti-body in the students just by viewing the film – without doing any of the actual charity work! By merely observing Mother Teresa's work, the students experienced the same physical benefits.

Our bodies are designed for helping others. The more you help others, the more it helps you! Helping others will help you to achieve a greater life! By focusing on the benefit of others, you can not only achieve balance in your life, you can improve your health and well-being. Helping others is just as important as exercising and eating a healthy diet. Imagine if you did all three during your *90 Day Run*!

Depending upon the goals you accomplish, your personal network will benefit from your achievements in some way. One of the first benefits they receive is to witness the process of Great Thinking. If you can do it, they can do it! When you show people how to *Think GREAT*, you will help them to think differently about achieving greatness in their own lives.

By accomplishing your personal goals, you will inspire them to do the same. Once people start to *Think GREAT* and accomplish their own goals, they start to realize that they can extend the achievement of greatness beyond their own personal needs, the needs of their personal network, and sometimes beyond the needs of people they personally know.

While there are numerous ways to help others achieve a greater life, they all have one thing in common: they provide you with personal benefits that can extend far beyond anything you could have ever imagined. Putting the needs of others above your own needs will change your life. Never run alone!

Chapter 12

Your GREAT Partner

Double Your Odds of Accomplishing Your Goals!

Having the support of your personal network will help you achieve greatness, but there is one member of that team who can guarantee it. Having a partner is different than having someone merely support you. A partner is in the trenches with you, every step of the way. A Great partner does not only support your *90 Day Run*, they are on it with you.

Imagine the power that can be created when two people, both with strong belief levels, partner up to help each other meet their goals. As the saying goes, "Two heads are better than one." Partnering up with the right person during your *90 Day Run* will have a significant impact on your results.

The best partnership is one where both partners are helping each other accomplish their own personal goals. As good as you think you are, everyone needs coaching to be great. Even Michael Jordan had a coach! Great partners are like personal coaches for each other, focusing on their big pictures.

Do not confuse support with partnership. There is a big difference between having someone assist you and having someone run the course with you. Anyone can say they support you. But a great partner believes in you enough to put their goals in your hands. That is both a tremendous compliment and responsibility.

WHO IS A GREAT PARTNER?

Many people make the mistake of choosing a partner they feel comfortable with. A great partner is not required to be a family member or even a close friend. They may not be the best choice to partner with because they are often good at pointing out your weaknesses, but seldom do they like it in return. Your partner can be a family member or close friend but hold the same high expectations for them that you would hold for anyone else.

The right person concept goes both ways. You will have an impact on your partner's results as well. Choosing the wrong partner will hold you back, making it harder to accomplish your goals. When you choose a partner, you are putting your goals in this person's hands for the next 90 days, so choose wisely.

The benefit that a great partner will provide to your *90 Day Run* is much more powerful than you may realize at first. Together, partners discover what is and is not working for their run. A great partner will help you to set higher expectations for yourself than you would set alone. They will help you to course-correct and break through barriers which normally would limit your ability to move forward.

During a *90 Day Run*, shared by two great partners, both individuals will be helping each other climb up the ladder to their goals, and move beyond the obstacles that prevented them from doing so in the past. A partner gives you the confidence of knowing that you are never alone on your journey.

Partners also provide each other with strategies and ideas to help shorten the distance to an important goal. They implement friendly competition and encourage trust and communication. After all, you are both sharing each other's most personal goals. A partner will help you stick to your schedule and minimize the number of actions you might miss. There is nothing better than commitment from your partner to keep you on track. If your goal requires you to show up at the gym, you may talk yourself into not going, but you are less likely to stand up your partner, right?

PARTNERSHIP = COMMITMENT

Good partners take their goals as seriously as you take yours. But great partners take your goals as seriously as they take their own. Partners encourage each other to push the limits. The synergistic energy between two committed partners will provide more horsepower to your *90 Day Run* than either of you could create alone.

Great partners not only generate this type of energy, they convert it into power by challenging each other to go the extra distance. Just as weight-lifters can lift more weight, with a partner 'spotting' them, a great partner will provide you with the power to accomplish more than you could have during any 90-day period by yourself.

Great partners will commit to the following actions to benefit their *90 Day Run*:

> **Completion** – Most people have a tough time sticking with something for 90 days. Great partners will keep each other on track to accomplish the main goal – completing the *90 Day Run* successfully.

> **Identification** – Most of us have no problem identifying our strengths. We usually need a little help with our weaknesses. A great partner will help you to identify improvements that will make you more effective.

> **Recognition** – Acknowledging the accomplishment of any goal, large or small, is powerful. But great partners remember to recognize each other for successfully taking the steps to get there as well. A pat on the back not only goes a long way but may come when it is needed most!

Partnerships help create a definitive direction, giving each of you the power to follow through and to continue taking action. Partners help each other to live up to their true potential.

A GREAT PARTNER WILL MAKE A GREAT DIFFERENCE

There are five ways that the power of a great partner will enhance your *90 Day Run*.

BELIEVE in Your Partner – A GREAT partner believes that you can do it. Knowing that someone believes in you will give you the extra edge you need to achieve greatness. It gives you the self-confidence to finally go after your goals. You will have an impact on your partner's ability to achieve greatness, so the greatest compliment is when someone believes in you enough to team up with you.

ENCOURAGE Your Partner – A GREAT partner encourages you to continue doing it. We all experience times when we feel like throwing in the towel. There will be moments when you question whether you can keep up. A GREAT partner will prevent you from failing by helping you to keep your big picture in mind and encouraging you to tap into your unused potential.

CHALLENGE Your Partner – A GREAT partner challenges you to do it better. You are already going for more than the status quo, and your partner knows when to give you that extra push. Greatness occurs by going above and beyond the call of duty, not standing at attention! A GREAT partner will not only keep you on track but will help you to gain more momentum.

SHOW Your Partner – A GREAT partner shows how to do it. For most people, their role models are not accessible. They may be movie stars or athletes. When you think GREAT and team up with a GREAT partner, you have a role model on call 24/7. You have a responsibility to your partner to give it your all, every day on your *90 Day Run*. What we do is always more important that what we say.

CARE about Your Partner – A GREAT partner genuinely cares that you get it done. They view their partner's goals as if they were their own! Honesty between partners is crucial and a GREAT partner cares enough to say it like it is. Sometimes, we all need to hear what we need to do in order to accomplish our goals.

No matter how much energy you put into accomplishing your goals, remember this: have fun with your partner. Do not forget to invest time with each other, discussing your goals and reinforcing the benefits of accomplishing them. Focus on keeping the energy level high in your partnership. Keep reminding each other that both of you are going after goals which are *life-changing and remarkable in magnitude and degree.*

THE BENEFIT OF A GREAT PARTNER

Having a partner will have more benefits than just helping to accomplish your personal goals. It can lead to achieving greatness in many facets of your life. In the early 1960's, two overweight boys were forced to run track by their teachers. They developed a friendship that continued throughout high school and the two began to dream of starting a food enterprise. In the late 1960's, the pair graduated from high school and signed up for a correspondence course from Pennsylvania State University.

They were both passionate about the direction their lives were heading in, but also shared some much bigger goals. They combined their savings of $8,000 and borrowed another $4,000. With $12,000, the partners opened up a shop in 1978. In 2000, their company was acquired for $326 million. The course on ice cream making paid off for Ben Cohen and Jerry Greenfield. The results of their partnership were far greater than just the outrageous flavors of ice cream the two friends had created.

Even though Ben & Jerry's ice cream soon had a cult-following, they wanted to achieve more than just great ice cream. Both of them had very strong personal values and an unwavering desire to give back to the community. Their desire was to mold Ben & Jerry's Ice Cream around their philosophies and not their philosophies around their business.

Their notion about creating a company which allowed their ideals to shine did not go unnoticed. In 1988, President Ronald Reagan awarded them with the title of U.S. Business Persons of the Year. Their partnership has achieved greatness in many areas. They established the Ben & Jerry's Foundation, which dedicates 7.5% of the company's pretax profit to communities through charitable organizations.

Personnel Journal awarded the company the *Optima's Quality of Life Award* in 1992 for creating an unusually nurturing workplace. Ben & Jerry's 700+ employees enjoy an on-site child care, a health club, and a generous profit-sharing plan. And the company encourages management to dress as casual as plant employees.

Ben & Jerry's Mission Statement has three parts: Product Mission, Economic Mission, and a Social Mission. Central to their business, "is the belief that all three parts must thrive equally in a manner that commands deep respect from individuals in and outside the company and supports the communities of which they are a part."

What if Ben & Jerry had never formed a great partnership?

A CHIP OFF THE OLD BLOCK

When I was a little boy, I wanted to be just like my dad. He worked many hours in the retail field to provide for us, so he was not able to spend much time with me. But I sure wanted to be just like him! When I became a teenager, I realized that we did not have a solid father-son relationship. He continued to put in long hours at work, and I spent most of my time with friends. I found that we really did not have that much to say to each other.

Our relationship started to improve when I joined the Marine Corps. He was genuinely proud of my service with the Marines. During the end of my tour of duty, my dad slipped into a coma for three weeks, due to diabetes. His condition was so critical that the Red Cross contacted my unit and requested that I be transferred to a base closer to home. He was not expected to live much longer.

This happened as my unit was shipping out for Gulf War I. Although my combat gear was packed and ready to go, I was transferred to Marine Corps Air Station El Toro, so I could be close to him. Against all odds, my dad recovered and eventually went back to work. But he returned as his company was down-sizing and letting go of some of the 'old-timers'. My dad was a very proud man and knew that his days there were limited. Because he was over 50, he found it difficult to find new work.

Soon after his recovery, I completed my tour of duty with the Marine Corps. My father found another job and I enrolled in college. He dedicated his free time to helping with my student films. He acquired props, prepared food, and found locations. As I continued my studies at Orange Coast College, he became more and more involved. When I screened my completed films for an audience, he helped me to rent out a room and made it feel like a real movie premiere. He even had a friend create posters for each of my 'blockbusters'!

When I transferred to the USC School of Cinematic Arts, my productions became more elaborate and my dad continued to stay on track with my goal. He traveled to the locations where I was filming and supported me in any capacity I needed. It was unspoken, but I had found my great partner.

I could count on him for anything. Our partnership caused us to be around each other much more than when I was younger. It was great communicating with him and finally getting to know my dad after all those years.

When I left the film industry to care for Gina, my father's finances were meager. He was commuting a long distance to a new job, and the drive was taking a toll on his body. After about a year in the financial services industry, I had achieved enough consistency in my sales that my dad and I would be able to partner once more and establish our own financial services office.

We had talked about our plans for a few months and I worked hard to get things set up. I wanted to rescue my dad from his job and long commute. But more than that, I looked forward to working with him every day. Our 'partnership' in film school was a great experience, so I knew the potential that this partnership could have. My dad was so excited that he bought a new suit for his first day of being in business with his son!

On Saturday, just two days before our first day in the office together, I received a frantic call from my mom. I rushed to their home to find the paramedics there already. He was having major complications due to his diabetes. My dad passed away the next day, the day before we would start our new partnership. We buried him in the suit he had just bought, with a picture of his grandsons in his pocket. It was a very difficult time for me. In fact, it had been only five months since Gina was released from the City of Hope, and she was still in her recovery phase.

Although I missed the opportunity for our partnership in the financial services industry, I will always have the memories of the projects we worked on together. My dad was a great partner, one who believed in me and put all of his efforts into helping me accomplish my goals. Not only were my films better due to our partnership, my life was better.

Great partners impact each other by sharing high levels of positive energy at all times. They will see the greatness in you, even when you cannot see it in yourself. A great partner will never let you down and will inspire you for the rest of your life!

A GREAT PARTNER HOLDS YOU ACCOUNTABLE

When we were kids, we had parents, teachers, and coaches holding us accountable for our actions. Perhaps that is why we try to achieve so much more at a young age. As we get older, we prefer to avoid accountability. Having a partner will bring that accountability back into your life during your *90 Day Run.*

You and your partner will not only be on your run together, you will help each other to enter the information into your G.P.S. You will focus on each other's Goals, Reasons, Expectations, and Actions. But most importantly, you will be Tracking each other's progress and results, measuring performance and collaborating on course-corrections. Having a great partner track your results will take your personal accountability to a whole new level.

You will be each other's navigator, coach, and inspiration. Partners can only have an impact if they communicate. Like most people, both of you will probably have demanding schedules. In addition to the actions required to meet your goals, you will need to balance your family, work, and personal activities as well. Productive time with your partner is important and must be scheduled into your G.P.S.

You will get more done by investing small amounts of time with your partner. While meeting face to face is always preferable, it may not be practical. I have had GREAT results by implementing two basic communication sessions each week.

Daily Call: A phone call at the end of the day to discuss the steps you have taken toward your goals. Invest about fifteen minutes to analyze areas you can improve. Talk about how it felt to take action or how it felt if you failed to take the required actions.

Weekly Meeting: A face-to-face meeting at the end of each week. Invest about thirty minutes to analyze your scheduled actions and results. Discuss your strengths and weaknesses, and any needed course-corrections.

Every call or meeting with your partner should have an outcome – moving closer to your goals. Having your G.P.S. and a copy of your partner's G.P.S. in front of you will help to keep you both on track. Do not forget to discuss your belief levels and the positive benefits you are already experiencing. Your goals rely on great communication from both of you! Your weekly meetings should be fun, and you should look forward to them. Try and do it over lunch or pick a unique setting, like a coffee shop, the beach, or a park. Conducting meetings in unique places can cause the creative juices to flow.

SILENT PARTNER

The power of two will create three! The mind is a powerful tool; when two great partners connect their belief levels, they will multiply their effectiveness, their physical energy, and their drive. When two great minds connect for a greater purpose, the results will be nothing short of amazing. This power is available to you and to your great partner.

The true benefit of having a great partner is that it adds extra power to your *90 Day Run* through *multiplication* rather than addition. But how is that possible? How does it work? Imagine that you are pursuing your personal goals on a *90 Day Run*. What good would it do for you to partner up with another person who is pursuing his/her own goals in the same 90 Day period? The math is still the same. It does not seem that any extra time is created by partnering up. So, what is the benefit?

You are right, two people cannot create extra time, but they can create extra energy through their 'Silent' Partner. When two Great Thinkers partner up and focus their individual belief levels on each other's goals, they create as much positive energy as if they had an additional partner: 1 + 1 = 3.

When two people with strong belief levels *Think GREAT*, they will have the ability to create the extra power needed for their *90 Day Run*. When two Great Thinkers get together to discuss the achievement of a greater life, they will produce more ideas and creative energy than their individual efforts ever could.

The power of a silent partner can provide additional impact. Undiscovered ideas will present themselves through this partnership.

MY GREAT PARTNER AND MY G.P.S.

Everyone needs someone they can truly count on. Great partners are in the field with you, not just cheering you on from the stands. They are committed to your greater purpose and you to theirs.

Your *90 Day Run* is *time*. You both have 90 Days, or 12 weeks, or 3 months, or 2,160 hours, or 129,600 minutes or 7,776,000 seconds to accomplish your short-term goals! However you view it, do not let a second of it get wasted. Most people fail to put enough of the right time into their day. Those who do not plan out their day, usually spend their day reacting to everyone else's plan.

Having a partner is like having a copilot, someone who will check your

G.P.S. while you control the plane! As you travel on the course to greatness, you will find that there are many possible routes. A properly developed G.P.S., reviewed daily with your partner, will take the guesswork out of your actions and help create precise answers.

Complete all of your steps together. Not only will you want to know each other's G.P.S. in detail, but you will benefit from the great energy created by designing them together. Two people can accomplish the same tasks in different ways. We are all unique. A great partner may offer you suggestions which will help you to accomplish your goals faster – saving valuable time!

Create shared goals and actions with your partner and schedule them into your Goal Planning Strategy. Being involved in each other's G.P.S. is essential to success. Helping your partner complete his/her G.P.S. and reviewing it daily is crucial. But you can add another dimension to your *90 Day Run* when you commit to each other's greater purpose and big picture.

Great partners will be there for each other to provide the support and motivation to overcome any obstacle together. And very importantly, partners will have the privilege of completing a *90 Day Run* and experiencing the feeling of accomplishing goals and achieving greatness – together!

Just as our drill instructors coached us by reviewing the information in our data books, a great partner will be able to coach you by reviewing the information in your G.P.S. Whether you enlist the support of a GREAT Partner for your *90 Day Run*, or not, you now have the information needed to accomplish your life-changing goals – no matter what circumstances you face!

Not only have you learned The 5 steps to Accomplishing Goals, but you understand the importance of Time Mastery and enlisting the support of people so you Never Run Alone.

You are ready to complete your G.P.S. for your own *90 Day Run*, and experience a life that is *remarkable in magnitude and degree.*

GREAT Exercises

Important People

While your partner will have a great impact on your *90 Day Run*, you have probably had many other people who have already provided significance in your life. Make a list of all of the people who have had an influence in your life and explain what they did.

My Personal Network

Make a list of people who you want to have in your personal network during your *90 Day Run*. Next to each of their names, identify what 'type' of person they are: Action Hero, Director, or Audience Member (No Critics in your personal network). Next, list out why they should be in your personal network. What positive benefit will they bring to the table that will enable you to accomplish your goals?

EXAMPLE:

PERSON	TYPE	REASON
Bob	Director	Can provide great ideas on investing
Mom	Audience	Will provide encouragement

Part IV

Your 90 Day Run Starts Now

Part IV

Your 90 Day Run Starts Now

Unlock a GREAT future!

Accomplishing your goals can be a lot like starting a new business. According to the U.S. Small Business Administration, "roughly 50% of small businesses fail within the first five years." Although different statistics explain how many actually fail, one common trait does exist. Companies that fail to develop and implement a strategic plan rarely stay in business.

Everyone can accomplish their goals, but not everyone will. Like businesses, people who fail to develop and implement a strategic plan rarely stay on track. By completing your *Goal Planning Strategy*, you are stacking the deck in your favor. You are proclaiming that your goals are important and that you will do whatever it takes to accomplish them.

Your completed G.P.S. will allow you to embark on a journey that you will complete. You will arrive at your destination and permanently change your life. Start by releasing the notion that all of the stars need to align to accomplish your goals. A perfect scenario never exists. Challenges will come, but your G.P.S. will allow you to course-correct along the way.

Do not over-analyze how your G.P.S. works. Instead, analyze how you are working on the actions necessary to accomplish your goals. Your G.P.S. is a tool to help you build a greater life. Completing it and reviewing it daily will make it a powerful tool during your *90 Day Run*.

A wise man once told me, "There's no hocus pocus, just focus." As with any goal, writing it down is a great step, but you must go beyond that first step. It will be up to you to make it a reality. Reviewing your G.P.S. daily will help to crystallize your plan and strategy for accomplishing your goals.

Your G.P.S. will not do the work for you. But it will help you to map out the work required to achieve a greater life. Put your heart into your plan, so your plan can get into your heart.

There is no ending when you think differently. It is the beginning of a new way of thinking and a new way of living. You will unlock the opportunity for a life more rewarding than you ever thought possible!

I want to congratulate you for not only reading *The GOAL Formula*, but for starting to *Think GREAT* in your own life. You have the power to change, the ability to enjoy all of the benefits of accomplishing your goals and experience the greatness in your life that you deserve.

I believe in you and your ability to accomplish greatness. I want to encourage you to start your *90 Day Run* NOW, and I want to challenge you to have a great impact in the lives of others. The *Think GREAT* Team is here to support Great Thinkers around the world. You can use the tools at our website: www.thinkgreat90.com.

Chapter 13

Your G.P.S. – Goal Planning Strategy

Put Together Your Personal Plan!

By launching your *90 Day Run* and tracking your progress with your G.P.S., you will gain control of your life by controlling your thoughts and actions. As a result, you will have the life you have dreamt about. It all boils down to what you think and what you do for the next 90 Days.

The following pages will give you a detailed description of the components of the G.P.S., show you an example of each completed page, and provide you with blank templates for your own G.P.S. Even though you are ready to move in a new direction, you may not know your exact destination. And that is OK. The main thing is that you want to get somewhere new in your life; somewhere better; somewhere GREATER!

Remember, Rome was not built in a day. In fact, it was not built in 90 either. Consistently reviewing your Goal Planning Strategy during your *90 Day Run* will keep you on top of your game. More than likely, you will accomplish many of your goals faster than you had originally mapped out. You may even develop new goals along the way.

Reviewing your G.P.S. helps you to win the war of focus. Most people fail to accomplish their goals because they cannot stay focused long enough! Let people in your life know what you are working on. Let your family and friends know your goals and the effort you are putting into accomplishing them. Let them know how much your goals mean to you.

Planning out each day will help you keep in mind any changes that have occurred in your life, which may require you to adjust your actions. As this step becomes more natural, you will start to identify the optimum times to perform certain activities. Life tends to throw curve balls once in a while, so, make sure you can be flexible and adjust your schedule to stay on track.

Each day can also be filled with interruptions that can divert you off course. Getting off course, even in a small way, can have a big impact over the course of 90 days. When we fired our rifles, our aim was crucial. Even if we were off by a fraction of a degree, the bullet may have missed the target by many feet. Remember to plan out your day the night before, to allow your mind to go to work even while you are sleeping!

A well-designed G.P.S. is beneficial when it is reviewed daily and analyzed for areas of improvement to make sure that nothing slips through the cracks. What justifies the additional time and energy you will spend reviewing and analyzing your G.P.S. daily? The increased chance for a greater life!

Step 1: Personal Contract

Verbal commitments are fine, but written ones last longer! Your Personal Contract highlights the commitment you are making to yourself and to the completion of your *90 Day Run*. Fill in your name, sign it, and date it. Make copies and post this page on your bathroom mirror, your desk, and in your car as a reminder of your dedication.

For an added impact have your great partner sign and date it too. Do the same for your partner.

Step 2: Overview

Your Overview will show the timelines for your *90 Day Run*, including your start date and completion date. Include in your Overview, a list of any long-term goals you must accomplish in order to achieve a greater life and identify which of the *Fantastic Five* categories they fall into. Your long-term goals will be broken down into smaller goals which you will add to the Short-Term Goals section.

You will also list who your partner is and establish your communication sessions for reviewing and discussing your G.P.S. together.

Step 3: Short-Term Goals

Use your Short-Term Goals section to identify all of the personal goals you will accomplish during your *90 Day Run*. Add in any of the shared goals that you and your partner want to accomplish together. Once again, list which of the *Fantastic Five* categories they fall into. Avoid the mistake of trying to tackle too many goals at the same time.

Do not forget to list your first goal as "Complete My *90 Day Run!*"

Step 4: G.R.E.A.T. Goal Sheet

Transfer each of your Short-Term goals to an individual G.R.E.A.T. Goal Sheet and list all of the information associated with each specific goal you expect to accomplish during your *90 Day Run*. Be specific. Instead of saying, "Lose weight," be detailed with how much weight you need to lose.

Instead of writing, "Buy a new home," write out something like this: "Buy a new, 3,000 square foot home, with a 3-car garage, 4 bedrooms, 3 baths, a pool, and a big front yard."

Step 5: Goal Status Sheet

This is where you will track your results and measure your progress for each of your short-term goals. This will require you to keep track of how close you are to the completion of your goal by tracking the '% Complete'.

Step 6: Daily Action Planner

Each day represents just over 1% of your *90 Day Run*. How you schedule your day will determine how successful you are in accomplishing your life-changing goals. As you schedule your new goal-related actions into your day, you will find it beneficial to account for both your day-to-day and your goal-related actions.

Avoid making your Daily Action Planner a 'To Do List.' They are boring and there is no life to them. Actions empower you!

Identify the 'Type' of each action: day-to-day or goal-related. For your day-to-day actions, put a 'D' under Type. For your goal-related actions, put a 'G' under Type. By identifying the type of actions that occupy your day, you will find that you can convert some of your day-to-day actions into goal-related actions 'D+G'.

Step 7: Daily Journal

The longer you make daily entries consistently, the greater the benefits are to your *90 Day Run*. A Daily Journal keeps you proactive and is a reminder of how serious your goals are to you. I have found that when you stop your journal entries, you soon stop your program. Your Journal allows you to keep track of your strengths and weaknesses. Knowing your history will allow you to change your future!

A motivational excerpt from *The GOAL Formula* will be on each page of your Daily Journal to inspire you!

Step 8: GREAT Achievements

Congratulations, you have successfully completed a life-changing step toward a greater life!

Each time you accomplish one of your goals, write it down on this form. It is time to celebrate!

The following pages provide you with examples of how I completed my G.P.S. There are also blank templates for you to complete and use during your *90 Day Run*.

GREAT examples of how to successfully complete your *G.P.S.!*

90 DAY RUN
PERSONAL CONTRACT

I, _____ *Erik Therwanger* _____ will accomplish my number one goal of completing my *90 Day Run*. I acknowledge that the accomplishment of my goals is extremely important to me and will also have a positive impact on everyone in my life.

I will *Think GREAT* during my entire *90 Day Run*. I will break bad habits and implement great habits. I will be a beacon of positive energy and will strive to inspire others to achieve greatness in their lives.

I understand that my *90 Day Run* will have some challenges, but I will stay persistent and consistent in everything that I do. During my *90 Day Run*, I will control my thoughts and actions. I will eliminate the option of failure.

Most importantly, I will pour my heart into my *G.P.S.* I will do the same for my GREAT partner. I will commit to reviewing my *G.P.S.* daily and focus my efforts on making my life GREAT!

_____ *Erik Therwanger* _____   *10/31/2009*
My Signature   Date

_____ *Gina Therwanger* _____   *10/31/2009*
My GREAT Partner's Signature   Date

90 DAY RUN
OVERVIEW

Start Date: _11/01/2009_   Completion Date: _01/31/2010_

In order to achieve a greater life, I will accomplish the following *Long-Term Goals*:

Long-Term Goals	Fantastic Five
1. *Eliminate all debt*	*Financial*
2. *Write a Book*	*Fun*
3. *Get in great physical shape*	*Fitness*
4. *Be a better parent*	*Family*
5. *Build a retirement fund*	*Financial*

My Great Partner: _Gina Therwanger_

Communication Sessions

Daily (Time): _8:00 pm_

Weekly (Day): _Saturday_   **Time:** _3:30 pm_

90 DAY RUN
SHORT-TERM GOALS

Personal Goals   **Fantastic Five**

1. COMPLETE MY 90 DAY RUN

2. Complete one chapter of my book per month   Fun

3. Plan three family outings   Family

4. Meet with a Financial Planner   Financial

5. Lose 25 pounds   Fitness

Shared Goals   **Fantastic Five**

1. Plan a 'Date-Night' once per month   Family

2. Find a long-term a Financial Planner   Financial

3. Pay off credit card - $4,200   Financial

4. Build a savings account - $1,000   Financial

5. Start a youth group at church   Faith

90 DAY RUN
R.E.A.T. GOAL SHEET #1

Goal #1: Lose 25 pounds.

Reasons: I want to lose this weight so I feel better and look better. I want to live longer and be able to have the energy to do more with my wife and kids.

Expectations: I will not give up. I will push myself everyday to stay on track. I will make my meals the night before so I don't have the need to buy fast food.

Actions: I will eat three healthy meals each day and I will have three small snacks in between meals to keep my metabolism going. I will exercise each day for at least 30 minutes.

Tracking: I will track my meals and exercise regimen each night using my Daily Action Planner. I will track my results each week by weighing in on Saturday morning!!!!

90 DAY RUN
GOAL STATUS SHEET #1

Goal #1: _Lose 25 pounds_

Timeline for Completion: _12/15/2009 – 75 Days_

In order to accomplish this goal I commit to eliminating these habits:

Eating fast food, drinking soda, eating late at night, being a couch potato.

In order to accomplish this goal I commit to adding these habits:

Preparing healthy meals each night for the following day, take vitamins daily,

exercise daily, and get enough sleep.

| 100% |
| 90% |
| 80% |
| 70% |
| 60% |
| 50% |
| 40% |
| 30% |
| 20% |
| 10% |

%
COMPLETE

Personal Network:

Louis B.

Kelli N.

Charlie H.

90 DAY RUN
ﾱILY ACTION PLANNER

01

	Time	Multiple Action Items	Type	Done
1.	7:30 am	Take the kids to school	D	☑
2.	8:30 am	Start work	D	☑
3.	12:30 pm	Eat a healthy lunch	D+G	☑
4.	6:00 pm	Eat healthy dinner with the family	D+G	☑
5.	8:00 pm	Review G.P.S. with my Great partner	G	☑
6.	8:30 pm	Exercise	G	☑
7.	9:00 pm	Prepare meals for the following day	G	☑
8.	9:30 pm	Put the kids to bed	D	☑
9.	9:45 pm	Write a couple pages in my book	G	◉
10.	10:30 pm	Go to bed	D+G	☑
11.				☐
12.				☐
13.				☐
14.				☐
15.				☐

	Time	Single Action Items	Type	Done
1.	1:00 pm	Schedule appointment with financial planner	G	☑
2.	1:15 pm	Pay bills – send $250 extra to credit card	D+G	☑
3.				☐
4.				☐
5.				☐

90 DAY RUN

JOURNAL

DAY 01

Strengths: _I stayed on track with my schedule about 95%._
Exercised on time and ate healthy meals. Spoke with my Great Partner for 15 minutes.

Weaknesses: _Ate lunch later than I wanted. Did not write any pages tonight._
I got home late from work and missed eating dinner with family.

How I can improve: _I will make up for the missed pages this weekend._
I will catch up at work to avoid missing any more goal-related actions!

GREAT thoughts for today: _It was great taking action towards my goals today._
Speaking to Gina about our G.P.S. gave both of us a tremendous boost of power.
I feel my confidence level growing.

Think GREAT today:
> Do not just sit back and watch others achieve greatness,
> Think GREAT and achieve it in your own life!

90 DAY RUN

SHORT-TERM GOALS

Congratulations!

	GOAL	DATE COMPLETED
1.	Picked our financial planner	11/10/2009
2.	Took family trip to the beach	11/13/2009
3.	Set up retirement fund	11/17/2009
4.	Completed first chapter of my book	11/27/2009
5.	Took family trip to amusement park	12/13/2009
6.	Completed second chapter of my book	12/24/2009
7.		
8.		
9.		
10.		

GREAT job!

90 DAY RUN

PERSONAL CONTRACT

I,_____will accomplish my number one goal of completing my *90 Day Run*. I acknowledge that the accomplishment of my goals is extremely important to me and will also have a positive impact on everyone in my life.

I will *Think GREAT* during my entire *90 Day Run*. I will break bad habits and implement great habits. I will be a beacon of positive energy and will strive to inspire others to achieve greatness in their lives.

I understand that my *90 Day Run* will have some challenges, but I will stay persistent and consistent in everything that I do. During my *90 Day Run*, I will control my thoughts and actions. I will eliminate the option of failure.

Most importantly, I will pour my heart into my *G.P.S.* I will do the same for my GREAT partner. I will commit to reviewing my *G.P.S.* daily and focus my efforts on making my life GREAT!

_____   _____

My Signature   Date

_____   _____

My GREAT Partner's Signature   Date

90 DAY RUN

OVERVIEW

Start Date:_____**Completion Date:**_____

In order to achieve a greater life, I will accomplish the following *Long-Term Goals*:

<u>Long-Term Goals</u>   **<u>Fantastic Five</u>**

1._____   _____

2._____   _____

3._____   _____

4._____   _____

5._____   _____

My Great Partner:

<u>Communication Sessions</u>

Daily (Time): _____

Weekly (Day): _____ **Time:** _____

90 DAY RUN

SHORT-TERM GOALS

Personal Goals   Fantasic Five

1. _____   _____

2. _____   _____

3. _____   _____

4. _____   _____

5. _____   _____

Shared Goals   Fantasic Five

1. _____   _____

2. _____   _____

3. _____   _____

4. _____   _____

5. _____   _____

GPS

90 DAY RUN

G.R.E.A.T. GOAL SHEET

Goal: _____

Reasons: _____
_____
_____
_____
_____

Expectations: _____
_____
_____
_____
_____

Actions: _____
_____
_____
_____
_____

Tracking: _____
_____
_____
_____
_____

GPS

90 DAY RUN

GOAL STATUS SHEET

Goal: _____

Timeline for Completion: _____

In order to accomplish this goal I commit to eliminating these habits:

_____
_____
_____
_____

In order to accomplish this goal I commit to adding these habits:

_____
_____
_____
_____

| 100% |
| 90% |
| 80% |
| 70% |
| 60% |
| 50% |
| 40% |
| 30% |
| 20% |
| 10% |

**%
COMPLETE**

Personal Network:

90 DAY RUN

DAILY ACTION PLANNER

	Time	*Multiple* Action Items	Type	Done
1.				☐
2.				☐
3.				☐
4.				☐
5.				☐
6.				☐
7.				☐
8.				☐
9.				☐
10.				☐
11.				☐
12.				☐
13.				☐
14.				☐
15.				☐

	Time	*Single* Action Items	Type	Done
1.				☐
2.				☐
3.				☐
4.				☐
5.				☐

90 DAY RUN

JOURNAL

Strengths: _____

_____

_____

_____

Weaknesses: _____

_____

_____

_____

How I can improve: _____

_____

_____

_____

GREAT thoughts for today: _____

_____

_____

_____

Think GREAT today:

*Greatness is absolutely attainable, no matter
what your personal circumstances are.*

90 DAY RUN

SHORT-TERM GOALS

Congratulations!

<u>**GOAL**</u>   <u>**DATE COMPLETED**</u>

1. _____   _____

2. _____   _____

3. _____   _____

4. _____   _____

5. _____   _____

6. _____   _____

7. _____   _____

8. _____   _____

9. _____   _____

10. _____   _____

GREAT job!

GPS

HOW WILL MY G.P.S. HELP ME TO ACHIEVE GREATNESS?

You have done a GREAT job! By inputting all of your information into your G.P.S., you are in a different league! In your quest for achieving greatness, you have already done more than 95% of the population. You are even starting to feel the impact of transferring your GREAT thoughts onto paper. Completing your G.P.S. will provide your *90 Day Run* with tremendous power, but nothing compares to the power of using it consistently.

Apply *The GOAL Formula* and experience your new life!

ACKNOWLEDGMENTS

My Deepest Gratitude

To my wife, Gina. Your desire to accomplish our goals, no matter what circumstances you faced, helped me to create this formula and strive for a greater life.

The United States Marine Corps – Semper Fi' and thank you for all of the valuable training I received which has shaped me into the person I am today.

About the Author

Erik Therwanger

Erik Therwanger began his unique career by serving in the U.S. Marine Corps as an air traffic controller. Leadership, honor, and integrity did not end after his four-year tour of duty; they became the foundation of his life, both personally and professionally.

After receiving the news that his wife had been diagnosed with cancer, Erik left his job in the entertainment industry, became her caregiver and started his new career in sales.

With no formal training, he began selling financial services. Relying on the strategies and techniques he learned as a Marine, he quickly became a top producer, recruiter, and trainer.

Erik returned to the entertainment industry and became the vice president of a media company in Santa Monica, CA. By building leaders, designing their strategic plan, and creating a dynamic sales system, he helped to raise annual sales by over 300%.

Erik's passion for helping others led to the creation of Think GREAT®. He successfully blends his leadership skills, his unparalleled ability to inspire and develop teams, and his wide array of strategic planning and sales experience, to provide practical solutions for individuals and organizations.

The Three Pillars of Business GREATNESS™ brings together the concepts from *The LEADERSHIP Connection, ELEVATE,* and *Dynamic Sales Combustion* to provide business leaders, and their teams, with a shared language of *leading, planning,* and *selling.*

Sharing his personal story and elite strategies, Erik's keynote speeches inspires audiences to strive for new levels of greatness. His interactive and powerful workshops highlight his step-by-step process for increasing results.

Erik delivers a compelling message that leaves a lasting impact in organizations, creating the necessary momentum to develop strong leaders, build visionary teams, and elevate sales results.

As the author of the Think GREAT® Collection, Erik has combined his challenging life experiences with his goal-setting techniques, to provide proven strategies to enhance the lives of others.

As a trainer and speaker for the spouses of armed services personnel, Erik is deeply aware of their challenges and sacrifices. To help support their education goals, Erik founded the *Think GREAT Foundation,* which is dedicated to awarding scholarships to the MilSpouse community. For more information, please visit:

www.ThinkGreatFoundation.org

www.ThinkGreat90.com

Please visit our website for more GREAT tools:

- Erik Therwanger's Keynote Speeches
- Workshops and Seminars
- Online Training Tools and Videos
- Register for the FREE Great Thought of the Week

More life-changing books in

- The LEADERSHIP Connection
- ELEVATE
- Dynamic Sales Combustion
- The SCALE Factor
- G.P.S.: Goal Planning Strategy
- The Seeds of Success for LEADING
- The Seeds of Success for PLANNING
- The Seeds of Success for SELLING

Printed in the United States
By Bookmasters